best
hikes
with
dogs
NORTH CAROLINA

best
hikes
with
dogs
NORTH CAROLINA

Karen Chávez

THE MOUNTAINEERS BOOKS

To Shelby, my best girl, my best friend, my best hiking buddy
And to my parents, Arlene Chávez and Jorge Chávez,
for loving Shelby as if she were one of their own

THE MOUNTAINEERS BOOKS
is the nonprofit publishing arm of The Mountaineers Club, an organization
founded in 1906 and dedicated to the exploration, preservation, and
enjoyment of outdoor and wilderness areas.

1001 SW Klickitat Way, Suite 201, Seattle, WA 98134

First edition, 2007

Manufactured in the United States of America

Copy Editor: Heath Lynn Silberfeld
Cover and Book Design: The Mountaineers Books
Layout: Elizabeth Cromwell/Books in Flight
Cartographer: Moore Creative Design
All photos by author unless otherwise noted.

Cover photograph: *Shelby*
Frontispiece: *Shelby scopes out the scene from a rock perch on Bartam Trail.*

Maps shown in this book were produced using National
Geographic's TOPO! software. For more information,
go to *www.nationalgeographic.com/topo.*

Library of Congress Cataloging-in-Publication Data
Chávez, Karen, 1970-
  Best hikes with dogs. North Carolina / Karen Chávez. — 1st ed.
    p. cm.
  Includes index.
  ISBN 978-1-59485-055-4
  1. Hiking with dogs—North Carolina—Guidebooks. 2. Trails—North
Carolina—Guidebooks. 3. North Carolina—Guidebooks. I. Title.
  SF427.455.C43 2007
  796.5109756—dc22
                              2007024920

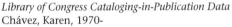

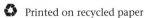 Printed on recycled paper

CONTENTS

Part 1: Hiking Tips for Dogs and People

Part 2: The Trails

Western North Carolina Mountains—Blue Ridge Parkway

Other Western North Carolina Mountains Hikes

Western Piedmont/Foothills Region

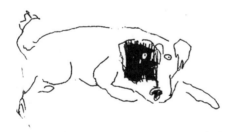

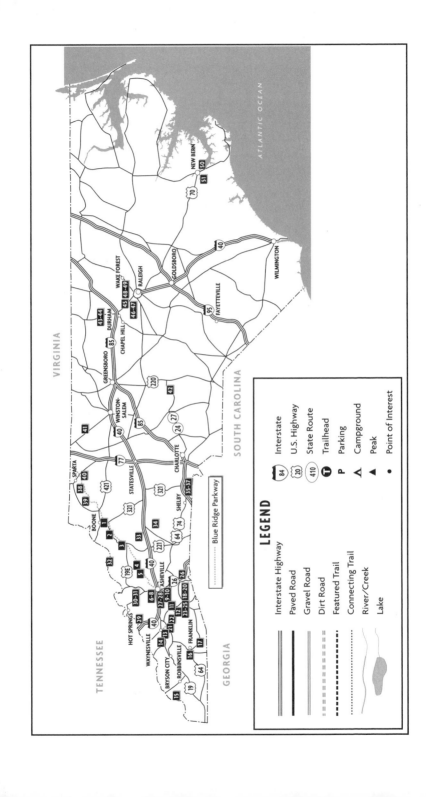

LEGEND

Interstate Highway	
Paved Road	
Gravel Road	
Dirt Road	
Featured Trail	
Connecting Trail	
River/Creek	
Lake	

Blue Ridge Parkway

84 Interstate
20 U.S. Highway
410 State Route
T Trailhead
P Parking
△ Campground
▲ Peak
• Point of Interest

ATLANTIC OCEAN

VIRGINIA

TENNESSEE

SOUTH CAROLINA

GEORGIA

NEW BERN

WILMINGTON

FAYETTEVILLE

GOLDSBORO

RALEIGH
WAKE FOREST
DURHAM
CHAPEL HILL
GREENSBORO
WINSTON-SALEM
CHARLOTTE
STATESVILLE
SPARTA
BOONE
ASHEVILLE
HOT SPRINGS
WAYNESVILLE
BRYSON CITY
ROBBINSVILLE
FRANKLIN
SHELBY

HIKE SUMMARY TABLE

Hike	Length of 3 miles or less	Strenuous climbing	Mountain views	River, creek, lake, or pond	Waterfall	Forested for most of trail	Off-leash permitted	Ledges or cliffs	Suitable for senior dogs	For trail-hardy dogs only
Western North Carolina Mountains—Blue Ridge Parkway										
1. Price Lake Loop Trail	•		•	•		•			•	
2. Tanawha Trail		•	•	•	•	•		•		•
3. Crabtree Falls Loop Trail		•	•	•	•	•				•
4. Old Mitchell Trail		•	•			•				•
5. Big Butt Trail		•	•			•			•	•
6. Craggy Pinnacle Trail	•		•			•		•	•	
7. Snowball Trail		•	•			•			•	•
8. Rattlesnake Lodge Trail		•	•			•			•	•
9. Mount Pisgah and Buck Spring Lodge Trails	•	•	•			•			•	•
10. Fryingpan Mountain Trail			•			•			•	
11. Graveyard Fields Trail		•	•	•	•	•		•		
12. Devils Courthouse and Little Sam Trail		•	•	•		•		•		•
13. Richland Balsam Nature Loop Trail	•		•			•			•	
14. Waterrock Knob Trail	•	•	•			•		•		•
Other Western North Carolina Mountains Hikes										
15. Joyce Kilmer Memorial Trail	•			•		•	•		•	
16. Rufus Morgan Falls Trail	•			•	•	•	•		•	
17. Bartram Trail—Jones Gap to Whiterock Mountain			•			•	•	•	•	
18. Cedar Rock Trail via Corn Mill Shoals and Big Rock Trails—DuPont State Forest	•	•	•	•		•		•		
19. Hooker Falls Trail—DuPont State Forest	•			•	•	•			•	
20. Triple Falls and High Falls Trails—DuPont State Forest	•	•	•	•	•	•				
21. Sam Knob Summit and Flat Laurel Creek Trails		•	•	•				•	•	

9

Hike	Length of 3 miles or less	Strenuous climbing	Mountain views	River, creek, lake, or pond	Waterfall	Forested for most of trail	Off-leash permitted	Ledges or cliffs	Suitable for senior dogs	For trail-hardy dogs only
22. Cold Mountain via Art Loeb Trail		•	•	•		•	•	•		•
23. Coontree Loop Trail		•	•	•		•	•			
24. Pink Beds Trail				•		•	•		•	
25. Cat Gap Loop		•	•	•		•	•			
26. Pulliam Creek Trail		•	•	•	•					
27. Pine Tree Loop Trail—Bent Creek Experimental Forest	•			•		•			•	
28. Carolina Mountain Trail—The North Carolina Arboretum	•		•	•		•			•	
29. Max Patch Trail			•						•	
30. Lovers Leap Loop Trail	•	•	•	•		•		•		•
31. Laurel River Trail				•		•		•	•	
32. High Bluff and Rhododendron Gardens Trails—Roan Mountain			•			•		•	•	
Western Piedmont/Foothills Region										
33. Sandy Cliff Overlook and Lake Channel Overlook Trails—Lake James State Park	•		•	•		•		•	•	
34. Shinny and Upper Falls Trails—South Mountains State Park		•		•	•	•		•		•
35. Pinnacle Trail—Crowders Mountain State Park	•	•	•			•		•		•
36. Crowders Lake Trail—Crowders Mountain State Park	•		•	•		•			•	
37. Tower and Backside Trails—Crowders Mountain State Park	•	•	•					•		•
38. Fern Nature Trail—New River State Park	•			•		•			•	
39. Summit and Rhododendron Trails—Mount Jefferson State Natural Area	•					•		•	•	
40. Stone Mountain Summit Trail—Stone Mountain State Park		•	•	•	•			•		•

Hike	Length of 3 miles or less	Strenuous climbing	Mountain views	River, creek, lake, or pond	Waterfall	Forested for most of trail	Off-leash permitted	Ledges or cliffs	Suitable for senior dogs	For trail-hardy dogs only
41. Jomeokee and Sassafras Trails—Pilot Mountain State Park	•		•					•	•	
42. Densons Creek Nature Trail—Uwharrie National Forest	•			•		•			•	
Eastern Piedmont/Coastal Region										
43. Occoneechee Mountain Trail—Occoneechee Mountain State Natural Area	•		•			•			•	
44. Buckquarter Creek Trail—Eno River State Park	•			•		•			•	
45. Sals Branch Trail—William B. Umstead State Park	•			•		•			•	
46. Inspiration Trail—William B. Umstead State Park	•					•			•	
47. Company Mill Trail—William B. Umstead State Park				•		•			•	
48. Falls Lake Trail (Mountains-to-Sea Trail)—Falls Lake State Recreation Area				•		•			•	
49. Woodland Nature Trail—Falls Lake State Recreation Area	•			•		•			•	
50. Beady Loop Trail—Neuse River Recreation Area, Croatan National Forest	•			•		•		•	•	
51. Island Creek Forest Walk—Croatan National Forest	•			•		•			•	

The Buckquarter Creek Trail meanders along the Eno River.

ACKNOWLEDGMENTS

Hiking with your dog—and writing about it—takes a small pack of dogs, and people. Special thanks to everyone who lent me a helping paw in this process, starting with my family.

First of all, thank you to my grandmother, Sister Marion Palmer Storjohann—a poet and an inspiration.

I especially need to thank my mother, Arlene Chávez, who served as my diligent, nitpicky copy editor, my helping hand, my crying shoulder; my brother, Glenn Chávez, who traveled from Tampa to hike the steep mountains with me and Shelby in the heat of a Southern summer; my sister, Dawn Chávez, who hiked mountain terrain with my twenty-five-pound nephew, Noah Rabin, strapped to her back; my brother, Mark Chávez, who was available 24/7 by phone to serve as my personal IT specialist. And thanks to my father, Jorge Chávez; my brother Brian Chávez; sister-in-law Barbara; nephews Luke, Jude, and Roman Chávez; nieces and nephew Naomi, Fiona, and Ethan Chávez; and brother-in-law Andrew Rabin, who were not able to hike with me but who all supported me in spirit.

Thanks also to my human hiking buddies and their dogs, especially Angie Newsome and Pat Hunt and their pup, Sammy; Mai Ly—one tough hiker; Holly MacKenzie, her son, Elliot, and their dog, Wesley; Leslie Ann Keller; and Jon Snow and his chocolate Lab, Talley. Thanks to all the state park, national park, and national forest staff and rangers who gave us their valuable time, advice, and expertise.

Special thanks to Phil Noblitt with the Blue Ridge Parkway, Frank Findley with the Nantahala National Forest, David Brown of DuPont State Forest, Mike Lambert of New River and Mount Jefferson State Parks, Janet Pearson of Pilot Mountain State Park, Betty Anderson of William B. Umstead State Park, Mike Carraway with the North Carolina Wildlife Resources Commission, and Julie Vidotto and Liz Malloy with the North Carolina Arboretum in Asheville.

Thanks to the members of the Carolina Mountain Club, especially Tom Sanders and Jorge Muñoz. And thanks to the staff at Charlotte Street Animal Hospital, especially Drs. Mark Ledyard and Anne Peden, not only for their help with the book but for their special care of Shelby for the past several years.

Thanks to Jay Schoon of the Trail Hound for his excellent suggestions and dog gear advice, and Lane Nakaji of Mast General Store for his dog hiking expertise and enthusiasm.

I also owe so much to all my friends and colleagues at the *Asheville Citizen-Times*, especially John Fletcher for his photography help and Jeff Ruminski and Bobby Bradley.

Jorge Chávez and his "granddog" Shelby practice sitting, staying, and other commands at home before hitting the trail.

PREFACE

Shelby—my somewhat middle-aged black Lab—is the center of my life.

She is the reason, literally, I get up every day. She is at my bedside each morning, letting me know it's time to get up and take her outside.

The center of Shelby's life, on the other hand, is not me. It is the great outdoors.

The sound of the wind knocking at the door, the sunlight streaming in through the skylight, the sound of the early morning songbirds, the squirrels teasing her through the window—these are the reasons Shelby gets up each morning, with her wet nose wiggling and sniffing, her ears on alert, that great tail swishing out of control.

Connecting my dog with her passion—to run, romp, and scavenge the woods—is what brings me happiness. This book has been the perfect way for me, a busy journalist, to get out of the office, into the woods, and connected with my dog. After the year we spent hiking across the rather wide state of North Carolina, up and down some of the highest mountains in the East, including the highest peak east of the Mississippi—Mount Mitchell—I feel Shelby and I have a tighter bond.

I don't have to tell her it is time to go hiking. She knows when I start putting her dog cookies in a baggie, and start arranging the gear in my pack, that we're off on another adventure. She runs to the door and waits for me to open it so she can run to the car, ready to jump in and go.

I learned that my dog will follow me anywhere. Rock ledges with sheer drop-offs, deep rivers with strong currents and slippery rocks, soaked trails with ankle-deep mud, paths so steep I have to scramble up using my hands, knees, and any available tree branch. And whether it is hot and muggy or cold and windy. Long trail or short. This means I have to be even more careful and considerate of the trails I choose. Just because they are okay for me, and Shelby will follow, doesn't mean they are the best for her.

I learned that she loves getting wet, no matter how cold it is. She is not crazy about walking on gravel. She can do without puppies and small-breed dogs. She is not afraid of mountain bikes (unfortunately). And she will come to my rescue when I trip, fall, or scream—a "rescue" that consists of smothering me with sloppy licks.

Shelby enjoys a moment of freedom in the outdoors.

I learned that after a long day outdoors, climbing, hiking, exploring, Shelby is content. She falls asleep quickly and deeply. And I know she is reliving the day's adventures of scouting out odors, sniffing pungent plants, splashing in streams, and getting muddy and dirty, by the sound of her noisy dreams.

What I learned from this past year: If you love your dog, you will take her hiking.

PART 1

Hiking Tips
for Dogs and People

Good Dogs Require Good Owners

If you want to lavish your dog with the best things in life, forget the posh doggy beds and gourmet dog food. Instead, get your dog outdoors and into the woods.

The great outdoors is what dogs live for. Everything we love about hiking—the greenery and fresh air, the smell of cedar and honeysuckle, the sweet sound of birdsong—these are all things that dogs love, maybe even more than we do. The outdoors is every kind of excitement to them—their iPod, Internet, cable TV, and Nintendo rolled into one.

But before taking your dog into the woods, you must make sure your dog is prepared and, more importantly, that you as the dog's protector and the ultimate responsible party are prepared. Know the topography of the trail and the rules such as leash laws, know the weather forecast, have the appropriate gear for you and your dog, and know how to take care of yourself and your dog in emergency situations.

The saying "The apple doesn't fall far from the tree" can be applied to dogs and their owners as well as to children and their parents. Ill-behaved dogs usually bear a shocking resemblance to irresponsible owners; overweight or unfit dogs usually live in a home where the people are overeating couch potatoes.

Angie and Pat take a break with Sammy on the Laurel River Trail.

The first step to being a good owner on the trail is knowing your dog. Not just her favorite kind of cookie, but her temperament, her likes and dislikes, her physical capabilities, her tolerance for heat and cold, and her reactions around people, dogs, wildlife, and unexpected situations. Most dogs are suited for hiking, not just big, high-energy dogs such as Labrador or golden retrievers. Most mixed-breed dogs will do great on the trail, and even Boston terriers and toy poodles can enjoy hiking. You just have to know what kind of trails and situations will best suit them.

For instance, a Chihuahua who has spent most of her life as a lap dog will not do well thrust all of a sudden onto a 10-mile, mountain climb over rocky terrain. If your dog has not been accustomed to hiking, try out some small, easy, level trails first to see how he will react and how far he can comfortably go.

A dog's physical fitness is important—a dog that spends most days eating and lying around the house or the yard will need more time to adapt to any hike more than 1 mile long or with any noticeable elevation change. Another factor is a dog's weight. Even a little beagle can out-hike an out-of-shape, overweight Lab.

Overweight dogs (and your veterinarian will tell you the sad, hard truth), just like overweight people, have to work harder to get up hills, which puts more stress on their hearts, bones, and joints. Be mindful of this, and do not try to push your dog harder than her abilities allow. Make sure your dog stays at a healthy weight and gets plenty of physical activity year-round so she is fit for hiking.

Also take your dog's age into consideration. At age nine or ten, most dogs are considered "seniors" and cannot move as quickly or agilely as they did as young pups. If you are just starting to take your dog out on the trail at this age, be considerate of her limited abilities. However, if your dog has spent a lifetime on the hiking trail, she will be able to handle more strenuous hikes later in life.

No matter how trail-hardy a dog is, however, you should keep him under a watchful eye. Dogs tend to wander: they can easily come across hazards such as drop-offs, snakebites, tangles with other wildlife, sharp rocks that can cut their paws, or rivers with strong currents. The best way to ensure your dog's safety on unknown trails is to keep her on a leash. Trails listed in this book that require leashes are well noted, but even in areas where leashes are not required, a responsible owner should always carry one. Good owners will also carry first-aid kits for their dogs and will know their dogs' health concerns before heading out on a hike.

Health Concerns for Your Dog

A common health concern for dogs that you should consider before an outing in the woods is weight and fitness level. While being overweight or out of shape can be easily addressed with some time spent feeding your dog a lower-calorie diet and getting him more exercise (including starting off with shorter, less strenuous hikes), owners should be aware of more serious health problems, including arthritis in older dogs, and hip dysplasia—a congenital disorder often found in large, purebred dogs such as German shepherds, Labrador and golden retrievers, and rottweilers. Hip dysplasia causes dogs to hop something like a bunny because their thigh bones do not fit properly into their hip joints.

Other health problems include breathing difficulties in dogs with short snouts, such as pugs and bulldogs. These concerns should not automatically preclude your dog from hiking, but they should be monitored closely. Safety and comfort for your dog should concern you as much as they do for any human in your hiking group.

Unlike people, dogs have no choice in where we take them—and if they are afraid, they might run away. They cannot tell us if they are in pain. If they are hurt, extremely thirsty or hungry, have a cut paw or injured leg, they might respond by running off, lashing out, or biting. It is up to you as the owner to constantly monitor your dog's health and signs of distress.

If you are uncertain if your dog is healthy enough for hiking, visit your vet to rule out any serious conditions. Otherwise, most young to middle-aged dogs should be fine for the average trail terrain—after all, they are naturally meant to be outdoors, on the prowl.

Even if your dog is young, strong, woods smart, and healthy, accidents always can occur. Following are some common injuries and ailments that dogs may encounter on the trail.

Hyperthermia or heat stroke and dehydration. Hyperthermia is an elevated body temperature that is a serious threat in summer in the midstate (Piedmont) and coastal regions of North Carolina. It even can be a problem in the western mountains at this southern latitude if you are overworking your dog in hot weather. You should avoid hiking with a malamute, husky, golden retriever, or other large-breed or long-haired dog in summer or during times of excessive heat and high humidity.

Dogs have a limited ability to dispense heat from their bodies and can overheat quickly. Always bring extra drinking water and foldable bowls for your dog, even on short hikes. Even if you have enough to

Collapsible, nylon water bowls are an essential piece of gear when hiking with dogs.

keep yourself and your dog hydrated, you are bound to encounter unprepared pet owners who do not think to bring water for their dogs, and you will want to share.

If you notice your dog is panting heavily and noisily, is staggering, or is unable to get up after lying down, this is a sign of heat stroke. Cool him down immediately by submerging him in a creek or lake, or dousing him with cool water, and give him plenty to drink before continuing. Even if a dog is not panting excessively, offer him a drink about every half hour to prevent dehydration.

Hypothermia. This extreme lowering of the body's core temperature, although rare in dogs, can be dangerous in the winter months—especially in the high elevations of North Carolina's western mountains—if a dog is left too long in frigid temperatures or falls into icy waters. Dogs should be warmed immediately, wrapped in clothes, and taken to a warm, dry shelter. Another cold-weather problem is frostbite on the tips of ears and noses or ice balls on the feet of long-haired dogs.

Vomiting or diarrhea. In the woods, this can often be caused by drinking contaminated water, so try to keep your dogs from drinking surface water. Dogs are susceptible to waterborne parasites such as giardia, just as humans are. Relatively speaking, running water and mountain springs are better than standing water, but they still pose risks.

If your dog has repeated vomiting or diarrhea, do not give him anything to eat or drink. If he has diarrhea, give him one or two doses of Imodium A-D to stop the diarrhea. But if it persists, you should cut short the hike and take your dog to a vet as soon as possible.

Cut, ripped, bruised pads. Foot care is extremely important on the trail. If a dog's pads or paws are injured and go long enough without treatment, you will be carrying her out of the woods. Always keep an eye on your dog's gait, watching for anything unusual, such as limping, favoring one leg for another, or what looks like walking on hot coals. These can all be signs of pad damage. Check pads often when hiking over rough, rocky terrain, gravel, icy or snow-covered trails, or hot sand or rocks.

Carry bandages and disinfectant in your doggy first-aid kit to treat and wrap wounds immediately. Even if the weather is not cold, pack dog booties to put on your dog to keep bandages in place or to prevent injury in the first place when walking over sharp rocks.

Cut or torn dewclaws. Dogs can cut or rip the dewclaw—the digit on the inner side of the front legs—on rocks, roots, or other sharp, thorny protrusions. These wounds often bleed heavily, so you should clean and quickly wrap them with a gauze pad and tape, and you should apply direct pressure if necessary to stop bleeding.

Sprains. Overanxious, rambunctious dogs, or puppies just being themselves, can bound a little too hard or jump a little too high and can sprain a leg muscle or joint just as humans do. If you notice your dog limping or favoring a leg and you can rule out a cut pad or other wound that needs bandaging, give your dog an appropriate dose (based on weight, about one pill per forty pounds) of aspirin or Bufferin to ease the pain, but do not give Tylenol or Advil, which are toxic to dogs.

Poisoning. Some of the most common household items that are toxic to dogs include chocolate, acetaminophen (the active ingredient in Tylenol), ibuprofen (Motrin or Advil), and antifreeze. Always keep your dog away from these substances (including that chocolate bar you brought for yourself).

Out on the trail, however, are more insidious poisons that can harm your dog. These include trail debris such as other hikers' garbage, dead animals or fish, or the branches of rhododendron and azalea trees, which are very common, especially in the mountains of North Carolina.

If your dog has ingested something potentially toxic, immediately administer syrup of ipecac to induce vomiting and prevent the substance from being absorbed into his system. If a couple of hours have passed, or if the substance (such as lye) can burn the esophagus, do not induce vomiting but get your dog to a vet as soon as possible.

Snakebites. Bites from poisonous snakes, such as rattlesnakes, can be a dangerous health threat to dogs. If your dog is wandering off trail or in deep grass and lets out a sudden yelp or a jump, immediately check him for fang marks, bleeding, redness, swelling, or fatigue. To delay absorption of snake venom into the bloodstream, clean the wound with Betadine, wrap it, and have him lie as still as possible. If you can carry your dog, this is the time to do it and get him to a vet quickly. Give your dog an antihistamine such as Benadryl to prevent anaphylactic shock.

Skunk spray. If your dog spends any amount of time outdoors, she will get skunked sometime in her life. Other than the smell and possible eye irritation, however, skunk spray is not a serious health threat. If you are far from home and do not have a gallon of tomato juice or dog shampoo in your backpack, the only way to handle skunk spray is to make sure to wash your dog's eyes and bear with the odor until you can get her a good scrub down with an application of skunk scent removal.

Permits and Regulations

For your own—and your dog's—safety and enjoyment while hiking, know the trail and all the regulations governing its use before heading out on a hike. This will help you to avoid tickets and fines, or driving a long distance only to learn something unpleasant, like the fact that dogs are prohibited on your chosen trail.

As a general rule, most national parks with large backcountry areas do not allow dogs on trails since these parks are often wildlife sanctuaries and dogs might chase, threaten, or disturb the native wildlife or, in turn, might be seen as prey by large animals such as coyotes or bears. Dogs are also not allowed in many of these parks because of their tendency to bark and disturb the wilderness atmosphere.

The ban on dogs in the backcountry is true of Great Smoky Mountains National Park, a beautiful wilderness area on the western edge of North Carolina with more than 800 miles of hiking trails. However, an exception in the dogless world of national parks is the Blue Ridge Parkway. This long and narrow national park site consists mostly of roadway, with numerous overlooks, picnic areas, and campgrounds along its 469

Take notice of all trail signs, such as this one in DuPont State Forest, for rules of the trail.

miles in North Carolina and Virginia. Much of the parkway is sandwiched between national forest land, however, so it offers many access points to trailheads that do allow dogs. Any time trails intersect parkway property, however, dogs are required to be on a six-foot-leash.

While U.S. Forest Service areas tend to have more lenient rules regarding dogs on trails, forest land is not a free-for-all. All four of the national forests in North Carolina require that dogs be under control at all times. Two—the Uwharrie National Forest and the Croatan National Forest—also require that dogs be on a leash on all trails.

The largest national forest in North Carolina—the Nantahala on the state's remote, western edge—and the Pisgah National Forest—just east of the Nantahala and also in the mountainous western part of the state—generally do not require dogs to be on a leash on backcountry trails, but they must be under voice control. However, this does not apply in front country areas such as developed campgrounds and picnic areas that are more heavily populated and where dogs often must be on a leash, although leash length is usually not specified. Whenever you are close to roads or parking areas, or around large groups of people, it is also a good idea to leash your dog for safety.

In addition, many state parks and state forests are adjacent to or near national forests and set their own rules governing pets. You must know where you are and which agency sets the rules. For example, some state game lands that exist within U.S. Forest Service areas have leash restrictions. According to the North Carolina Wildlife Resources Commission's Game Lands rules, "Except for authorized field trials, dogs may not be trained or allowed to run unleashed between April 1 and August 15 on any game land located west of Interstate 95. Dogs also may not be trained or allowed to run unleashed during daylight hours on dates when special hunts are scheduled for the Disabled Sportsman Program hunts on these game lands. Additional restrictions apply to some bear sanctuaries and game lands."

In all state parks, recreation areas, and natural areas, six-foot leash laws apply. Owners are also required to clean up after their pets and, to protect local plant life or native wildlife, must not let their pets stray off marked trails. Some parks do not allow dogs in the backcountry or in swimming areas. Dogs are usually never allowed in buildings, such as bathhouses and visitor centers.

Hunting is a popular activity across the state, and a hunting season of some sort, from small game to deer and bear, takes place from early fall through May. Gun season for deer in western North Carolina generally runs for three weeks from the end of November to the beginning of December. Gun seasons for deer in other parts of the state may begin as early as mid-October and continue to January 1. While hunting is prohibited in state parks and in national parks, many of the trails in these areas adjoin state game lands and forest service land, without visible fences or borders. While hunters are required to wear blaze orange during hunting season, other outdoor recreational users are not, but it is strongly advised that they do so. This goes for dogs as well. Pet shops and outdoor outfitters

sell blaze orange vests and bandanas and bells to wear on collars to help distinguish dogs from game animals. Know when and where hunting is allowed. For optimum safety, avoid hiking with your dog in game lands during hunting season, or hike on Sundays, when hunting is prohibited in the state.

Also be aware that in some counties and municipalities, dog owners must be able to show proof that their dogs have received a rabies vaccination (in some places, dogs must wear a rabies vaccination tag) and, in some cases, that they are licensed.

Signs such as these designate areas that are open to hunting.

Go Lightly on the Land

Dogs, with their little bodies and soft paw pads and tendency to never toss food wrappers on the ground, naturally tread more lightly in the woods than humans ever do. Unfortunately, dogs are often looked upon as nonnative species that do not belong on hiking trails. Dog owners need to be conscious of this and go the extra mile to reduce almost to zero the impact they make while hiking with their dogs.

Practicing Leave No Trace ethics while hiking, camping, and back-packing is something everyone should do to help preserve the integrity and beauty of natural areas. But dog owners need to be extra careful to oversee their dogs' behavior on the trail.

Leave No Trace is a land use program promoted by the Leave No Trace Center for Outdoor Ethics (*www.lnt.org*). Based in Boulder, Colorado, the international nonprofit is dedicated to assisting outdoor enthusiasts in preventing or reducing their impacts when they hike, camp, bike, back-pack, or participate in any outdoor recreational activity. The Leave No Trace program includes seven principles of outdoor ethics, which can be applied to people hiking with their dogs.

1. Plan ahead and prepare.

This means knowing the rules and regulations for the area you plan to visit; bringing the proper gear, food, water, and clothing you will need for you and your dog; and minimizing impact by avoiding trails at times of high use. Your dog can help by carrying in a special doggy day pack the extra water or food she will need.

2. Travel and camp on durable surfaces.

Staying on "durable surfaces," such as established trails and roads, will help to reduce impact in the backcountry. Even when allowed to be off leash, dogs should also be kept close to their owners and on trails to avoid damaging plant life and to reduce soil erosion on fragile slope areas. Hikers should walk in single file in the middle of the trail.

3. Dispose of waste properly.

If you are an outdoors enthusiast, no doubt you have heard the saying "Pack it in, pack it out." Reduce waste even before starting your hike by repackaging food, batteries, film, and such out of their plastic and paper wrappers and place them in reusable containers so you have nothing to dispose of in the backcountry. If you do have any food wrappers or other trash, take it out of the woods with you. This includes leftover food and food waste, such as banana peels and orange rinds. While these organic materials will break down over time, that is unlikely to happen before many people pass by and are greeted by unsightly garbage piles.

It is also extremely important to dispose properly of solid human and dog waste to avoid pollution of water sources, to avoid other people or other dogs finding it, and to minimize the possibility of spreading disease. Such waste, along with toilet paper, should be buried in catholes dug out with a small garden trowel and should be six to eight inches deep, four to six inches in diameter, and at least 200 feet from water, campsites, and trails. Catholes should be dug in inconspicuous places where other people will be unlikely to walk or camp. Cover and disguise the cathole when finished.

If you need to wash dishes, carry the water 200 feet away from streams or lakes and use small amounts of biodegradable soap, then scatter strained dishwater.

4. Leave what you find.

"Take only pictures, leave only footprints." Most all state and national parks prohibit the removal or destruction of any plant, animal, artifact, rock, or mineral. This means no matter how pretty the wildflower, or how

Bluets are some of the many spring wildflowers that bloom along the Fryingpan Mountain Trail, but trail etiquette and Leave No Trace principles call for leaving everything in nature as you find it.

much you want that rock for use as a paperweight, what you find must stay put. In certain cases, exceptions exist for activities such as blueberry picking, but this is usually limited to what you can consume yourself.

The idea is to pass through a natural area with as little impact as possible so that no one knows you were there. This applies to dogs as well: do not let them dig excessively or trample flowers or plants.

5. Minimize campfire impacts.

In most state and national parks in North Carolina, and in wilderness areas in the national forests, campfires are prohibited. In places where campfires are allowed, use established fire rings, keep fires small, and only use firewood found on the ground and that can be broken by hand. Burn down all wood and coals to ash, put out campfires completely, then scatter cool ashes. Embers left burning can have disastrous effects, especially under windy or extremely dry weather conditions. It is better to use a backpacking stove instead of a fire for cooking and flashlights or lanterns for light.

6. Respect wildlife.

This is a particularly important principle to observe when you are hiking with your dog. Avoid and do not approach wildlife, especially during winter or when they are mating, nesting, or raising young.

Dogs can be seen as predators and can have a disturbing effect on native wildlife, even causing wildlife to react aggressively. Never feed wildlife; this can damage their health, alter their natural behaviors, and expose them to predators and other dangers.

Protect wildlife—and yourself—by storing food and trash securely.

7. Be considerate of other visitors.

Respect other visitors and the quiet and stillness that they come to the outdoors to enjoy. Yield to others on the trail (especially if you have a dog) and avoid making loud noises. When you are with your dog, keep him from disturbing the outdoor experience for others. Keep your dog on a leash in areas where it is required, when many people are on the trail, and also if someone requests that you put your dog on a leash. Being considerate also means maintaining the peaceful atmosphere of the outdoors by keeping your dog from barking. (More on canine trail etiquette follows.)

Good Canine Trail Etiquette

Good dog manners on the trail start with you. In many beautiful hiking areas, including national parks, such as the Great Smoky Mountains National Park in the western mountains of North Carolina, dogs are prohibited on hiking trails. In areas where dogs are allowed, the rules can be very restrictive, including keeping dogs on leashes no longer than six feet. Even with these restrictions, many people would rather not see any dogs on the trail. To prevent further limits on allowing dogs to enjoy the outdoors, you should always know and follow the rules, and even go the extra mile to make sure your dog does not bother people or wildlife. Aim for the Emily Post pooch award by following these eight rules of canine trail etiquette.

1. Make sure your dog is trail trained.

Some dogs tend to get overstimulated on the trail—there are so many new smells, sights, and sounds—and they can respond with abnormal or "bad" behavior, much like children who become hyperactive at a playground.

If you do not know how your dog will behave in the woods, start off with a short hike, maybe on a less crowded trail, and see how she responds.

2. Limit the number of dogs in your hiking party to two.

Even if you are hiking with several people, no more than two dogs should be in your group—any more than that can quickly turn into an unruly pack and appear intimidating to other people, even dog lovers. A pack of dogs also becomes more unpredictable, especially when they encounter other dogs or wildlife on the trail. You might suddenly find yourself in the middle of a zoo. This many animals hiking together also has potential for greater impact to the trail and backcountry, which goes against the next rule.

3. Leave no trace.

This canon of hiking and backcountry etiquette applies to both humans and dogs. Do not pick, trample, or damage plant life or allow your dog to do any similar damage. You and your dog should stay on trail whenever possible to prevent further erosion or disturbance to rare or fragile plant life off the trail. Do not make shortcuts or switchbacks up and down steep sections of trail where none exist. Most dogs will go off trail to relieve themselves, but you should always clean up the solid waste to prevent the

Grayson and his dog, Sasha, take in the impressive view from a rocky summit in the Pisgah National Forest. To prevent accidents, dogs should be on leashes whenever you are hiking near ledges or dropoffs.

spread of disease and to prevent other people and dogs from stepping in it (see Go Lightly on the Land for more details on leaving no trace).

4. Yield to trail users without dogs.

This includes hikers, horses, other pack animals, and mountain bikers. It is better to give people without dogs the right-of-way than to get into a possible physical or verbal entanglement. If you encounter dog lovers, they will usually ask to pet your dog or make welcoming and encouraging comments. In many cases, dogs can be a good conversation starter among hikers. But if you meet people who do not like dogs, it is better to give them a wide berth and let them pass you.

5. Always leash your dog when encountering other people and dogs on the trail.

Even in areas where leashes are not required, it is common courtesy to leash or restrain your dog when passing others. Some trails are extremely narrow, and people might become easily intimidated by passing an unleashed dog in a confined space, especially a large, nosy dog.

Although you might have a dog with a friendly nature, in the unfamiliar surroundings of the forest with strange sightings and scents of people suddenly emerging from around a bend or behind some trees, your dog might react unpredictably or become protective of you and be aggressive toward strangers. Be especially careful of small children—a large dog could easily knock down a child on the trail.

When parties with dogs come across each other on the trail, both parties should leash their dogs until they have had a friendly sniff hello and are safely past each other. However, there will always be discourteous dog owners who let their dogs bound off leash and out of control. You should still leash your dog in such situations and continue moving away from the unleashed dogs. The exception is if the dogs are extremely aggressive, in which case it would be easier for your dog to protect himself off leash.

6. Obey the rules of the trail.

Trail rules are often in effect for your safety, as well as for the protection of the natural environment. They also serve to keep your pet safe. In places where dogs are prohibited on trails, such as Great Smoky Mountains National Park, the rule is enforced to protect the native wildlife, which includes a healthy population of black bears, as well as to keep your dog safe from the bears.

In other areas, such as North Carolina's state parks, dogs must be on a leash at all times—these are often high-traffic areas with many other people and dogs. Keeping dogs on leashes limits the potential for conflict, accidents, and unpleasant situations.

Packing out what you pack in, cleaning up your dog's waste and disposing of it in an approved garbage bin or a properly prepared cathole, staying out of restricted areas, and not harming and not letting your dog harm plants and other wildlife are all common examples of trail rules that will help to keep natural areas safe, pristine, and enjoyable for future generations of hikers—and if followed, they will continue to allow the privilege of hiking there with your dog.

7. Clean up after your dog.

Always carry plastic bags for picking up and carrying away your dog's poop. You never know when the need might arise, and it is never acceptable to leave dog droppings where they fall. Even in wilderness areas, you should treat dog waste as you do human waste, burying it at least six inches deep and at least 200 feet from the trail or water source, or packing it out with you until it can be disposed of properly.

8. Walk softly and carry a leash.

Most people do not drive many miles from cities to head into the forest to hear noise. This includes the peace-shattering sound of humans yelling to each other and the loud, disturbing din of barking dogs. Be sure your dog is not a chronic barker before going on a hike. If she does bark at a wild animal, a stranger on the trail, or for some other reason, stop the barking as quickly as possible to maintain the natural peace and quiet of the wilderness. If the only way to keep your dog from barking or in other ways disturbing the native plants and wildlife is to have her on a leash, that is the way you should hike with your dog.

Myths and Misunderstandings About Dogs

Dogs make great hiking companions, and they also serve unknowingly as trail guides and security guards. Dogs have much better hearing and sense of smell than do humans, and if you watch them, their sudden stops, turns, and sniffs can lead you to spot birds, other wildlife, or pretty wildflowers you might otherwise miss. Most dogs will instinctively protect their owners from other people or wildlife on the trail.

However, some myths and misunderstandings about dogs on the trail persist, arising out of fears people have, possibly from a past traumatic experience with a dog or from a general ignorance about dogs and their behavior.

Following are some of the common myths about dogs in the woods.

1. False: Dogs don't belong on the trail.

Yes, some people believe this. If not outdoors, then where do dogs belong? Being outside, especially in natural settings, sniffing, running, hunting, rolling around: these are all natural instincts in a dog's genetic makeup. Sadly, many dogs spend most of their lives locked up in apartments or houses, with a twice-a-day, fifteen-minute bathroom break and walk around the block.

Imagine if that were your life. Dogs cannot even be entertained by TV, the newspaper, the radio, or the Internet. They live for the outdoors. Not to mention, they need exercise, both for good physical health and mental stimulation. When people wonder why their dogs chew their shoes and furniture and get into the garbage can, it is most often the humans' fault. Dogs are just following their naturally curious noses and trying to burn off some energy by getting exercise that is so often lacking in their lives.

Dogs need more than a couple of pee breaks during the day. They need to run and fetch, jump and splash, and run some more. Dogs need lots of exercise. The bigger the dog, the more exercise he needs. And if you give dogs the proper amounts of exercise, you will reward yourself—dogs who burn off energy outdoors will be calmer at home and not feel the need to tear up the house.

Of course, dogs also need discipline outdoors, especially on public trails around other people, other dogs, and wildlife. In most cases and on

Dogs of all sizes can hike. Small breed dogs such as this one do better on shorter trails, such as the High Bluff Trail on Roan Mountain.

most trails, dogs should be on a leash, for their own safety and to make sure they do not chase a bear or other wild animal.

The more you walk outdoors with your dog, on a leash, the more you establish yourself as the leader, making it easier to control your dog's behavior outdoors. Even on the trail, you should make sure your dog walks beside or behind you, rather than in front and pulling you, as if she were the pack leader. Always stop your dog's bad behavior immediately (rather than yelling at him twenty minutes later, when he will have no idea what you are yelling about), do not let him chase wildlife, and do not let him jump on other people or dogs you meet. If you can show that your dog is well behaved on the hiking trail, this will help dispel the myth that this is a place where dogs do not belong.

2. False: Dogs damage trails.

Most dog breeds—except for supersized breeds such as Great Danes and Rhodesian ridgebacks—are much smaller and lighter than the average person walking in the woods. Naturally, this means they put less pressure on the environment and make less of an impact on the trail. And dogs don't wear boots—they traipse lightly across the forest floor with their little pads. Unlike humans, dogs have never been known to carve their initials into tree trunks.

As long as dogs are with responsible owners who do not allow them to run off trail, trample delicate plant life, or leave their droppings on the trail, dogs do not harm the woods or the trails any more than people do.

3. False: Dogs disturb wildlife.

Dogs operate on instinct, and most—if given the chance—will want to pursue the instinct to chase rabbits, squirrels, cats large and small, deer, turkeys, and even bears. Young wild animals are particularly vulnerable because dogs can catch them easily. The key lies with owners properly training and restraining their dogs. With the proper training and conditioning, dogs should obey their human companions, should not run off, and should come when called. If you have a dog that has to chase anything that moves, it is your responsibility to keep her restrained on a leash to protect the native wildlife.

If people follow the rules of the park, forest, or natural area where they are hiking, their dogs should not cause any more stress to the local wildlife than children or adults do when walking in the woods.

Glenn and Shelby head out on the Fern Nature Trail in New River State Park.

4. False: "That (small) dog won't hunt."

If you are not from the South, you may not have heard that saying (it means something doesn't sound quite right). Here, the myth is that small dogs do not make good hikers.

Any dog can hike—he just needs a trail to match his ability level, the same as with people. Some breeds are not built for long hauls or steep, rocky terrain—the short little legs of dachshunds are not going to be able to climb most trails in the mountainous region of North Carolina without wearing out quickly—but they would have a fun time on plenty of short, flat trails.

Dogs with short snouts—and short legs—such as pugs, are not well suited for arduous climbs either, but just like any other dog, they enjoy getting outdoors and they need the stimulation of fresh air and forest sights, smells, and sounds. Just about any dog breed will make a great hiking buddy, given the right trail.

5. False: Dogs spread disease.

In the United States, most dogs are house dogs. They live with us in our homes and often snuggle up with us in bed. We care for them as if they were our children, feeding them well (sometimes too well), giving them baths, and making sure with annual trips to the veterinarian that they get appropriate shots and other medical care.

We make sure our dogs are healthy, happy, and disease free. Unless a dog contracts a disease from a rabid animal—usually a wild animal such as a raccoon—they do not spread diseases.

Owners are responsible for cleaning up after their dogs and must dispose of waste properly to further ensure that disease is not spread this way.

The Essentials

The first step to having a safe and fun hiking trip with your dog is to make sure you have the proper gear and clothing for yourself. Whenever you go for a hike—no matter the distance—always bring a backpack or fanny pack to carry the essentials so you can have your hands free. This is especially important when hiking with a dog. In most instances, dogs need to be on a leash, so holding a leash in one hand while holding a water bottle or other gear makes hiking cumbersome.

For safety, you should always hike with at least one other person since you or your dog may encounter many unforeseeable dangers, such as twisted ankles, injuries to you or your dog, falls, dehydration, allergic reactions, sudden storms (which are especially prevalent in the high elevation mountains of western North Carolina), disorientation in unblazed or overgrown trails in wilderness areas, or meeting up with unsavory characters. Having a human hiking buddy along will increase the chances of getting home safely.

Gear for You

When dressing for a hike, dress for success. The best way to dress for a day on the trail is in layers. This will get you through almost any kind of weather, from spring through summer, fall, and winter.

Start by wearing a base layer of a synthetic, moisture-wicking material (not cotton). Cotton, including tee shirts and jeans, soaks up sweat and precipitation and does not dry quickly, which can lead to skin irritation at the least and hypothermia at the worst.

The second layer should be a long-sleeved shirt (depending on the season) and, on top, a water-repellent jacket. The colder it is, the more insulating layers, such as fleece or wool jackets, you should wear under the top layer. As you get hiking and warm up, you can peel off layers.

Footwear is also important on the hiking trail. For relatively flat, easy trails, sturdy walking or running shoes are fine. But on trails with rocky terrain or hikes with noticeable elevation gain (usually any hike in the mountain region), your feet and ankles will need extra support so you should wear hiking boots, preferably made of waterproof material.

Ten Essentials: A Systems Approach

1. **Navigation (map and compass or Global Positioning System [GPS]).** Most of the hikes detailed in this book are on established trails. But trails can be altered by weather and trail markers can become obscured. You should always carry a map with as much detail as possible—preferably a topographic map showing elevation changes—and a compass whenever hiking in the woods, and know how to use them. Hiking clubs and outdoor outfitters usually offer classes in navigation. GPS devices, which use satellites to pinpoint your latitude and longitude, are now becoming more popular and more affordable. But the signals can sometimes be weakened by high rock walls or heavy tree cover, dying batteries or extreme cold. Be sure you understand how to properly use a GPS before relying on it in the woods.

2. **Sun protection (sunglasses and sunscreen).** Your eyes are your guides. Always carry sunglasses, even on cloudy days. The sun can cause near-blinding glare in the coastal and Piedmont regions of the state as well as on exposed ridge tops in the forested western mountains. And even in winter, sunburn at high elevations can occur. Protect your skin and especially the delicate areas on your face with sunscreen.

3. **Insulation (extra clothing).** No matter how many weather forecasts you consult before heading into the great outdoors, Mother Nature can always trick you. The best way to prepare for any type of weather is with layers. Dress in and bring extra moisture-wicking, synthetic clothing, since it is breathable

and quick drying. Stay away from cotton. Not only can extra layers be added or removed as the temperature fluctuates or the harder you hike and sweat, but extra clothing can protect against wind, thorny shrubs, or insects.

4. **Illumination (headlamp or flashlight).** A lightweight lamp or flashlight is indispensable in the backcountry. Darkness comes faster and denser in the woods with heavy tree cover. Always bring extra batteries, or a flashlight rechargeable by hand crank.

5. **First-aid supplies.** Always carry a first-aid kit that includes bandages, antiseptic, disinfectant ointment and adhesive tape for cuts and abrasions, moleskin for blisters, pain killer such as aspirin or acetaminophen, antihistamine such as Benadryl for allergic reactions, anti-nausea medicine and any necessary prescription medications. Instant cold packs also come in handy to reduce swelling.

6. **Fire (fire starter and matches or lighter).** These are necessary to start a fire for warmth or possibly to send an emergency signal if you become lost, as well as to cook food or boil water.

7. **Repair kit and tools (including knife).** A knife or a multi-use tool is vital in the backcountry for a variety of tasks such as repairing gear, cutting line or rope, and preparing food.

8. **Nutrition (extra food).** Calories burn up quickly on the trail. Besides bringing picnic-type food that you plan to eat within an hour or two, such as a sandwich and fruit, you should always pack extra food that will keep for much longer, preferably high-energy food such as protein bars or gorp with dried fruit and nuts.

9. **Hydration (extra water).** You will get thirsty. Even if you plan to hike in an area with a lot of rushing rivers or streams, you should never drink surface water without first purifying it with a purification system, chemical filter, or by boiling. When you are hiking, your body will require more hydration than usual. The suggested amount of water to bring is at least 2 quarts per person per day. You should also bring a water purifier.

10. **Emergency shelter.** An emergency tent or space blanket can come in handy in the event of getting lost or injured and

having to spend a night in the woods. It can also be a lifesaver in the event of sudden storms as protection from the cold, wind, or rain by lessening the chance of hypothermia.

Canine Ten Essentials

The gear and supplies you need for a hike with your dog are what you would normally bring for a day of hiking for yourself, plus a few canine-specific extras. The most important are current identification tags with your dog's name; current immunization tags, including rabies; and your name, address, and phone number. If your dog were to run off, these tags would be essential in retrieving him. Another good option is to have a microchip implanted.

You should also have these ten essentials for your dog:

1. **Obedience training.** Before you set foot on a trail, make sure your dog is trained and can be trusted to behave when faced with other hikers, other dogs, wildlife, and an assortment of strange scents and sights in the backcountry.

Shelby wears a doggy backpack to help carry her water and snacks. Dogs can comfortably carry about 25 percent of their weight.

2. **Doggy backpack.** Lets the dog carry his own gear, up to one-quarter of his weight.
3. **Basic first-aid kit** (see A Doggy First-Aid Kit).
4. **Dog food and trail treats.** Bring more food than your dog normally consumes since she will be burning more calories than usual. If you end up having to spend an extra night in the woods, you will need to feed your dog. Trail treats serve the same purpose for the dog as they do for you—quick energy and a pick-me-up during a strenuous day of hiking. Even if a hike is not that long, dogs often will walk at least twice as far as people by running ahead and back, and treats are also handy in helping to retrieve a wandering dog.
5. **Water and water bowl.** Extra drinking water and a collapsible bowl for your dog are essential. You can never be sure that you will encounter a spring or reliable drinking source along the trail.
6. **Leash and collar or harness.** Always carry a leash, even if hiking in areas where leashes are not required. Even if your dog is absolutely trained to voice command and stays at heel without a leash, sometimes leashes are required by law or just by common courtesy. A six-foot, nylon leash is lightweight and easy to pack away, compared with the heavy and bulkier retractable leashes. Also, many national and state parks and other hiking areas require that leashes be six feet long or less.
7. **Insect repellent.** Be aware that some animals, and some people, have strong negative reactions to DEET-based repellents. Before leaving home, dab a little DEET-based repellent on a patch of your dog's fur to see if he reacts to it. Look for signs of drowsiness, lethargy, and/or nausea. Restrict repellent applications to those places the dog can't lick—the back of the neck and around the ears (staying clear of the ears and inner ears) are the most logical places mosquitoes will be looking for exposed skin to bite.
8. **ID tags and picture identification.** Your dog should always wear ID tags, and you should carry the picture identification in your pack. If your dog gets lost, you can use the picture to make flyers and handbills to post in the

surrounding communities. Strongly consider having a microchip implanted. To do this, a vet injects a tiny encoded microchip under the skin between a dog's shoulders. If your dog ever gets lost and is picked up by animal control, or is taken to a vet's office, a quick pass over the dog's back with a hand scanner will reveal the chip and allow the staff at that shelter or hospital to identify your dog and notify you. Most veterinarians and animal shelters automatically scan every unknown dog for microchips.

9. **Dog booties.** These can be used to protect the dog's feet from rough ground or harsh vegetation. They are also great for keeping bandages secure if a dog damages his pads.

10. **Compact roll of plastic bags and trowel.** Pack plastic bags to pick up dog waste on trails, as well as hand sanitizer, and bring pet or baby wipes for removing the unknown substances your dog might decide to roll in. When conditions warrant, you can use the trowel to dig a small hole several inches deep, deposit the dog waste, and fill in the hole; otherwise, pack it out.

If hiking in bear country, such as the black bear habitat of much of western North Carolina, you and your dog should wear bear bells. If you are trekking through national forest land or state game lands where hunting is allowed, you and your dog should also wear blaze orange vests during hunting season.

If you are going on an all-day or extra-long hike, consider getting a doggy day pack. These specially designed backpacks with straps that fasten under the dog's belly and across her chest are a good way to let her help. Dogs like having a job and getting loud, positive praise as they trek along carrying their own food and water. And having your dog share in the packing will leave more room in your pack for extras such as a camera, guidebooks, or binoculars.

Generally, dogs can carry one-quarter of their weight, so an eighty-pound Lab could comfortably carry about twenty pounds, but you should not have him carry that much on a first outing. Rather, build up first with an empty pack so he can get used to it, then slowly add more weight on subsequent outings, making sure it is evenly distributed on his back. Have a knowledgeable salesperson at an outdoor outfitter or pet store help you pick out an appropriate dog pack.

A Doggy First-Aid Kit

Always pack a pet first-aid kit. Having one is necessary, even if it has only the bare-bones essentials. For a complete, comprehensive canine first-aid kit though, anyone heading into the wild with a canine companion should carry the following essentials for the dog's first aid:

Instruments

- Scissors/bandage scissors
- Toenail clippers
- Rectal thermometer (a healthy dog should show a temperature of 101°F when taken rectally)

Cleansers and disinfectants

- 3% hydrogen peroxide
- Betadine
- Canine eyewash (available at any large pet supply store)

Topical antibiotics and ointments (nonprescription)

- Calamine lotion
- Triple antibiotic ointment (bacitracin, neomycin, or polymyxin)
- Baking soda (for bee stings)
- Petroleum jelly
- Stop-bleeding powder

Medications

- Enteric-coated aspirin or Bufferin
- Imodium A-D

Dressings and bandages

- Gauze pads (4 inches square) or gauze roll
- Nonstick pads
- Adhesive tape (1-inch and 2-inch rolls)

Miscellaneous

- Muzzle
- Dog booties
- Any prescription medication your dog needs

For extended trips, consult your vet about any other prescription medications that may be needed in emergency situations, including these:

- Oral antibiotics
- Eye/ear medications
- Emetics (to induce vomiting)
- Pain medications and anti-inflammatories
- Suturing materials for large open wounds

Trail Hazards

Even though a tranquil walk in the woods might appear to be the most innocuous of settings, being unprepared can cause trouble. Know what to do in the case of water dangers, encounters with wildlife, and sudden or extreme weather changes.

Water

One of the best traits a hiking trail can have, from a dog's point of view, is water. Whether it is a lake, a pond, a river, or a trickle of a creek, most dogs are drawn to the shiny reflection of water in the sun, the movement, the sound, the cool taste on their tongues, and the mystery of what lurks beneath the surface.

But dogs should not be allowed to drink heartily from any surface water since the parasite *Giardia lamblia,* as well as bacteria and viruses, might be present, even in remote wilderness areas. Untreated water can cause serious illness, stomach cramping, and diarrhea in dogs, just as it can in humans. Giardia cannot be killed by iodine treatment and water must be boiled before drinking.

Trying to prevent your eager, curious, and thirsty pooch from drinking when he comes upon water on the trail is a bit unrealistic. But do try to

Booties help keep dogs' paws warm and dry in winter and are also good for rocky terrain.

Big Laurel Creek is a treat for dogs hiking along the Laurel River Trail. But owners should watch dogs carefully around swift-moving water such as rivers and waterfalls.

steer him away from any standing water, such as ponds and bogs, which will have more bacteria buildup than will running streams. Always bring extra clean drinking water and a collapsible nylon water bowl for your dog to keep him hydrated, safe, and happy.

Speaking of water hazards, dogs might also get into trouble near waterfalls and rain-swollen streams. Even people—who should know better than to climb on the extremely slick rocks around waterfalls—do not always employ common sense and continue to be careless around falls, and every year fatalities from climbing on slick rocks occur in North Carolina. Dogs will have an even harder time resisting the urge to get closer to the powerful streams of waterfalls, so leash your dogs above waterfalls and watch them carefully in pools below them.

Also use caution when walking along riverbanks, especially after a heavy rain has raised river levels. Rocks here can be slippery, and a wrong step can send a dog swimming—against her will—down a rapid current.

Do not attempt to cross high or flooded rivers, especially if the water is above a footbridge or if there is no bridge. It is always better to turn back and try the hike another day than to lose your life, or your dog's, trying to stick to a plan.

During winter hiking, rivers can be especially dangerous. Rivers that ice over can seem deceptively solid, but dogs who trot out on frozen rivers can easily cause a crack and fall beneath the ice.

Wildlife

Bears. American black bears live and roam in many areas of eastern and western North Carolina (there are none in the Piedmont). Bears are abundant in Great Smoky Mountains National Park. This is one of the reasons dogs are not permitted on hiking trails in the park. Bears also live throughout the rest of western North Carolina and are protected from hunting in certain bear sanctuaries.

Though they are rare, bear attacks have happened in North Carolina. Bears can be unpredictable if they are hungry, if they are mother bears defending their cubs, and if they themselves feel threatened.

To reduce the chances of having a problem with a bear, always keep your dog on a leash in bear country and don't allow her to run free. Most incidents of dogs being hurt or killed by bears are the result of the dog attacking or approaching the bear. Your dog might pick up a bear scent and want to chase it. If she is unrestrained, there is no way to prevent this. Talk loudly with your hiking party members, or to your dog, and have your dog wear bear bells to let bears know you are coming through. Bears tend to avoid contact with humans, especially in places where hunting is allowed. Hike in groups during daylight hours, avoiding dusk and evening when bears are more active. Bears tend to approach humans only in places where people leave out food or trash, such as trail shelters and campgrounds, since the bears see this as an easy food source. Always keep a clean camp, do not clean fish at camp, do not eat in your tent, and keep food and garbage stored in designated bear boxes.

Here are some guidelines to follow if you do find yourself, with or without your dog, face to face with a bear:

- Do not approach the bear.
- Stop and make noise to let the bear know you are there.
- If the bear leaves, proceed slowly, and with caution. Most often, the bear will leave when it becomes aware of human presence. However, in some situations an individual bear has become so accustomed to people that it won't leave or show any fear of people or dogs.

- If the bear does not leave, you should back up slowly and then walk away in that direction.
- If the bear starts to approach or charge at you, make yourself appear bigger by holding out your arms or opening your jacket and act aggressively by shouting loudly at the bear. Even throwing things such as water bottles at the bear may intimidate it.
- People who live and walk in bear country can carry pepper spray (available at outdoor outfitter shops). Though rarely used, it can be effective in deterring bears at close range if they show no fear and approach within a few feet of you.
- If you are attacked by a black bear, the best response is to fight back (punch, kick, scream, gouge). Playing dead is not advisable with black bears.

Fire towers, such as this one at the summit of Fryingpan Mountain, offer great views, but dogs should not be allowed to climb them. They can become afraid to descend, and small dogs can easily fall through the wide spaces between steps.

Bobcats. Although rarely seen, bobcats do inhabit a range of habitats across North Carolina. If you are hiking in areas where bobcats have been spotted, always keep your dog on a leash so that she will not pick up their scent and give chase. If you encounter a large cat on the trail, do not run—this will trigger a predatory chase response. Keep your dog on a leash and close by your side. A cat is less likely to attack two animals at once. Try to back away slowly.

Coyotes. Coyotes inhabit the entire state of North Carolina. They have been known to roam in packs and to attack small dogs, but this occurs more often in residential areas and backyards than in the forest. Coyotes, much like any wildlife, tend to avoid humans. And people walking with dogs will seem even more of a threat. To avoid contact with coyotes when in the woods, as with bears, make noise to alert them of your presence. In most situations, the scent of a dog will keep wildlife out of your path.

Snakes. Northern copperheads and timber rattlesnakes are among the poisonous snakes that inhabit the state, and they are usually found in high grassy areas, stone piles, or rocky areas. Water moccasins are found in the eastern part of the state. Watch dogs carefully if they start sniffing around in tall grass or in rocky areas, and get them out of harm's way if you hear the warning shake of a rattler's tail. A poisonous snakebite can be fatal to dogs, and keeping your dog on a leash will largely prevent any encounters with snakes.

Weather

The weather might just be the biggest danger when hiking with your dog, or the biggest hindrance to having an enjoyable time. But don't blame the weather—be prepared by knowing the forecast before heading out on the trail, and be prepared with the proper gear and clothing.

Cold, Snow, and Freezing Rain

The quickly changing weather in North Carolina is one of the biggest concerns for hikers and their dogs. In the western mountains, where altitudes reach well over 6000 feet, cold weather and snowstorms can blow in suddenly, even in spring, and strong winds and thunder and lightning storms can barge in with barely any warning.

Every year in early spring, when hundreds of hikers set out on the 2176-mile journey along the entire Appalachian Trail, some people are always in need of rescue when they hit the high country of North Carolina's Great Smoky Mountains. Those who did not plan properly are ill suited for the sudden snows that can cover trails, freezing rains that can soak clothing and boots, and freezing temperatures that can lower body temperatures and cause life-threatening hypothermia.

The layering approach to dressing for the weather is the best way to be prepared. For a base layer, always wear synthetic, breathable clothing that wicks moisture away from the skin and dries quickly. Wear a second layer for warmth, such as lightweight wool or fleece, and a wind- and water-resistant outer layer. Rain gear for dogs is also available in outdoor outfitter shops and pet stores. Dog booties for keeping paws warm and preventing frostbite are important to have in case of sudden storms.

In the mountain elevations above 5000 feet, hypothermia can even be a problem in summer when sudden rainstorms can quickly lower body temperatures of hikers who are not properly dressed. One of the symptoms of hypothermia is disorientation, so it might be even more difficult to find your way out of the woods when you are cold and wet.

Dressing in layers will help when you meet with unexpected weather conditions. Cold weather and storms can appear suddenly, even in summer, on Mount Mitchell, the highest peak in the East.

Wind

A cool mountaintop breeze might feel nice while you are hiking in summer, but cooling winds can actually be deadly in cold, wet weather. Winds that routinely gust up to hurricane force in the high country of western North Carolina, such as Mount Mitchell and the Grandfather Mountain range, are no joke. If it is cold and raining, wind will speed up the loss of body heat from humans and dogs, which will increase the chances of hypothermia.

Always pack a wind-resistant outer jacket. If you do find yourself in a windstorm, cut the hike short and head for shelter.

Dangerously high, hurricane-force winds can be a problem in late summer and early fall in the coastal region. You should never attempt to hike when a coastal storm is forecast.

Lightning

Lightning can be a serious threat in summer, especially in the mountains, on balds, or on open summits, since it seeks to strike the highest point. If you can hear thunder, you are within striking distance. A strike can cause burns, heart attacks, and even death.

If you do get caught in a thunder and lightning storm, try to get off the mountaintop down to lower ground, and seek shelter as quickly as possible. Do not crouch under trees, especially tall trees, for protection. Trees are magnets for lightning strikes, even if there is higher ground above the trees.

Since many dogs are afraid of thunder and lightning, they might react by running off or acting strangely. They should be kept on a leash during a storm and taken quickly to shelter, away from the noise.

Heat and Humidity

Stifling heat, compounded by sticky humidity, is a danger during the summer months in the Piedmont and coastal regions, but temperatures can also soar in the mountains. Always bring plenty of drinking water and keep yourself and your dog well hydrated on the trail. If you are hot and thirsty while hiking, you can bet your dog in her hairy coat is even hotter and thirstier. Dogs will not tell you if they are thirsty or getting overheated, and they will push themselves to keep up with and please their owners. Always check your dog's vital signs and offer her water at least every half hour, or more often, depending on the temperature and the difficulty of the trail.

Knowing the forecast before you head out, planning ahead, and bringing the proper gear are essential to safe hiking.

Using This Book

Best Hikes with Dogs: North Carolina is intended as a starting point on the road to outdoor fun and exercise with your dog. It is written to give you an idea of the diverse hiking opportunities appropriate for dogs across the state.

Keep in mind that trails are changing, closing, morphing, and expanding even as you read this book. Storms can blow down trees or wash away hillsides, forcing land agencies to close trails. Construction can temporarily close or reroute hiking paths. Dangerously icy road conditions, a common occurrence in the high country areas in western North Carolina, can close off hiking access roads such as the Blue Ridge Parkway for weeks at a time during winter.

Conditions can change quickly in nature, so before heading out on any hike, check with the state or national park or forest office. Phone numbers and websites, when available, are provided with each hike description to make it easy to obtain the most up-to-date information.

The trails in this book are arranged geographically, starting in the west and heading east. Since the 469-mile-long Blue Ridge Parkway (half of which runs through North Carolina before heading into Virginia) cuts through some of the most scenic mountain topography, just made for hiking, one section is devoted to trails accessed from the parkway. These are listed in geographical order and by milepost, in ascending order, from north to south.

The next section is devoted to other trails in the western mountains region, including the two largest national forests in the state—the Pisgah National Forest and the Nantahala National Forest. Other trails in state forests and state parks are also found here. The next sections comprise the Piedmont and coastal areas.

An elevation profile for hikes with an elevation gain of 150 feet or greater, topographic map, and reference to a USGS map accompany each trail description. When available, references to more up-to-date or site-specific maps are also included since many USGS maps are only current as of the 1950s or 1960s. Often, such man-made features as roads, campgrounds, visitor centers, and trails are not visible on the older maps, especially for newer state parks.

The Blue Ridge Parkway—part of the National Park Service system—can be seen snaking through the mountains from the top of Mount Pisgah.

The beginning of each hike contains a block of information that will help you to quickly determine if this is a suitable hike for you and your dog. Each information block includes distance and *hiking time,* which are based on the average person's gait of two miles per hour. However, this is greatly variable depending on how much time you want to spend stopping to take pictures or enjoy a picnic, or how much time the dogs want to spend splashing in a river or sniffing mushrooms and flowers.

The *high point* is also noted for each trail, along with *elevation gain,* which is the difference from the highest to the lowest point on the trail. This is not cumulative elevation gain, which can be much greater over the course of a trail.

Difficulty of hikes ranges from easy—generally less than three miles and less than 500 feet of elevation gain; moderate—three to five miles with 500 feet or more elevation gain, and some added obstacles such as rock hopping of rivers; and difficult—usually at least three miles with significant elevation gain and sections of precarious footing or scrambling with the use of hands and feet. Keep in mind that the difficulty rating is merely a guideline and should be considered along with the distance and knowing your own hiking ability, as well as your dog's.

Rules and fees define the regulations regarding leashes and any other pertinent information related to dogs.

The *contact, and getting there* entries denote the closest city or town; the state or national park, national forest, or other land management agency where the trail is located; the corresponding phone number and website to refer to for the most updated information; and driving directions from the nearest town.

How the Trails Were Selected

North Carolina is a great state for hiking, for both people and dogs. The rather wide nature of the state, stretching nearly 1000 miles from the western Tennessee border to the Atlantic coast, gives it three distinct geographic regions: the western North Carolina mountains; the Piedmont; and the coast.

The western mountains are the epicenter of hiking in North Carolina and contain some of the highest peaks east of the Mississippi, including the highest—Mount Mitchell (6684 feet)—and many forests, parks, peaks, cliffs, waterfalls, and grand vistas. For that reason, many of the hikes found in this book are located in the west.

For those familiar with this part of the United States, one hiking area that obviously has been omitted is the sprawling Great Smoky Mountains National Park. This most visited of U.S. national parks straddles the North Carolina–Tennessee border. While the hiking is superb there, including sections of the Appalachian Trail, the park does not allow dogs on any of its backcountry trails.

Other regions of the state have great hiking high points, though, including areas close to some of the urban centers, such as Raleigh, Charlotte, and Winston-Salem. Following are the criteria used to select the best hikes with dogs.

- The hiking area must be friendly to dogs, both in official regulations and in the type of terrain. The trails must be easily passable for dogs, without any need for fording deep rivers (although in some cases, rivers are shallow and narrow enough for most dogs to wade or swim across), climbing ladders, or having to hoist dogs over cliff faces, for example. The trails also must be used primarily for foot traffic, not open to motorized vehicles, and, in most cases, off-limits to horses and mountain bikes to limit the potential for collisions with dogs.

Jack, a springer spaniel, enjoys a family outing to Max Patch Mountain.

- The trails have to offer a real hike—that is, an excursion involving boots, a day pack, a pack of trail mix, some exertion, and a walk over natural terrain, rather than a stroll through a city park on a paved walkway. Dogs dig the real deal: the smell of dirt and the feel of grass and leaves underfoot.

Mai and Shelby head carefully down a staircase on the Crabtree Falls Loop.

- Trailheads have to be easily accessible by motorized vehicle, with a suitable parking area. They have to be on public lands, whether national park or forest, state park or forest, or other publicly owned property. Although some areas have access or parking fees or defined hours of access, none requires permission from a private landowner.
- Even though this book is all about dogs, each hike has to have an element of interest for the people tagging along. Whether the payoff is a lovely shaded forest glen, a leisurely stroll along a stream, a mesmerizing waterfall, a stunning mountain view, the remains of a historic homestead, spectacular spring wildflowers, or the seasonal splendor of fall leaf color, each hike has a little something for the humans.

- If a trail crosses multiuse areas where hunting is allowed, the text has to note that clearly so that hikers know when to avoid those places and to be prepared by keeping dogs on a leash and using blaze-orange doggy vests or collar bells. While it is ideal to hike trails only where hunting is prohibited, that would limit many beautiful national forest and game land areas.

Enjoy the Trails: Get Involved

The miles of trails in North Carolina seem endless. Can you imagine trying to maintain them all? Trails need constant maintenance to stay in top shape, as we do for our physical health. Trails get overgrown, eroded from overuse or heavy rains, blocked by rock slides or windstorms toppling trees. Often, trail maintenance is the last item on the agenda for land management agencies, which are stretched thin on money and personnel.

Most trails in county, state, and national parks and forests are kept humming, manicured, and alive through the sweat equity of local conservation groups and hiking clubs. Volunteering with some of these groups is a good way to help keep the trails open for future human and canine generations.

Some trail maintenance groups that work in North Carolina are listed in the appendix.

A Note About Safety

Safety is an important concern in all outdoor activities. No guidebook can alert you to every hazard or anticipate the limitations of every reader. Therefore, the descriptions of roads, trails, routes, and natural features in this book are not representations that a particular place or excursion will be safe for your party. When you follow any of the routes described in this book, you assume responsibility for your own safety. Under normal conditions, such excursions require the usual attention to traffic, road and trail conditions, weather, terrain, the capabilities of your party, and other factors. Keeping informed on current conditions and exercising common sense are the keys to a safe, enjoyable outing.

The Mountaineers Books

The Bartram Trail in the Nantahala National Forest is well-maintained by volunteers with the Bartram Trail Society.

PART 2

The Trails

WESTERN NORTH CAROLINA MOUNTAINS— BLUE RIDGE PARKWAY

1. Price Lake Loop Trail

Loop: 2.3 miles
Hiking time: 1.5 hours
Best time to hike: Year-round, Blue Ridge Parkway road conditions permitting
High point: 3410 feet
Elevation gain: 35 feet
Difficulty: Easy
Rules and fees: Dogs must be on a leash no longer than 6 feet; campground fee to camp overnight
Map: USGS Boone
Contact: Blue Ridge Parkway Headquarters, 828-271-4779; Price Lake Campground, 828-963-5911; automated road and weather conditions, 828-298-0398; *www.nps.gov/blri*

Getting there: From Blowing Rock, take US 321/221 south to the Blue Ridge Parkway. Take the parkway south about 2 miles to milepost 297.2. Turn left at the sign for boat rentals and the amphitheater, and park at the Boone Fork Overlook parking area, overlooking Price Lake. The trailhead is to the right of the trailhead sign, down the ramp by the boat dock.

Your dog will love you for this hike, and you can give yourself a pat on the head as well for embarking on this trail. Price Lake Trail encircles 47-acre Price Lake in the middle of Julian Price Memorial Park. Although man-made, Price Lake is a pristine, sparkling jewel that perfectly complements its rugged mountain surroundings. It sits in the high country of western North Carolina near the towns of Boone and Blowing Rock on the Blue Ridge Parkway. In addition to the postcard-pretty lake, the 4300-acre park offers the largest—and possibly the most scenic—campground on the parkway, open May through October with 180 sites, a large picnic area, trout fishing, nonmotorized boating, and access to many hiking trails in the imposing shadow of Grandfather Mountain.

It is an ideal weekend getaway spot, but even if you just have a couple of hours, this is a must-do hike. It's perfect for nearly any dog and especially so for water lovers such as Labs, since plenty of easily accessible areas will invite your dogs to take a dunk in the lake. Short-legged dogs

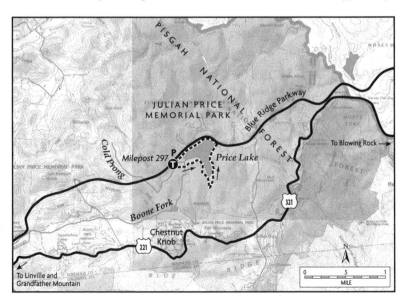

such as dachshunds, older dogs, and those who are not adept rock climbers will enjoy the level terrain. The 2.3-mile trail hugs the lake for the entire loop without any noticeable elevation change, so the hike will be over, sadly, before you know it.

Start by entering a rhododendron forest. You will definitely get the feel of being in a remote forest even though you will be on a wide, level, well-marked, and well-tamped trail, built to allow wheelchairs access to the fishing pier. At 0.2 mile, come to the first bridge, which crosses over Cold Prong, and a bench on the other side. Red maples, tulip poplars, rhododendron, and mountain laurel frame the lake.

At 0.4 mile, arrive at a bridge over Boone Fork where you can look back across the lake dotted with lazy-moving canoes and rowboats to the launch ramp where the trail began. Continue winding through the forest to the accessible fishing pier at 0.7 mile. There is easy lake access for dogs to take a swim, but if people are fishing, a splashing dog is probably not the best company. Many people stop here to fish or sightsee and turn back, but if you continue the loop, you will encounter many more openings onto grassy, lakeside banks where dogs can take a dip in the lake and you can sit, picnic, or daydream.

Kani and Ellenburg with their poodle and Maltese mix, Sofi, enjoy a rest stop while hiking around Price Lake.

Just after the fishing dock, the trail loses its well-groomed appearance and becomes more rustic, narrow, muddy, and rocky. At 1 mile, come to a boggy area at the southern arm of the lake, fed by Laurel Creek, and cross a boardwalk. This trail can be accessed year-round, as long as the Blue Ridge Parkway is open, with season-specific treats, such as trillium, bluets, buttercups, and other early spring wildflowers; blooming rhododendron in June; goldenrod in late summer; and the rich reds, yellows, and oranges of the fall foliage show.

At 1.65 miles, the trail emerges abruptly from the woods onto the Blue Ridge Parkway. Turn to the left, being careful to keep dogs away from the road, and cross the dam toward Price Lake Overlook, where you will find great views of Grandfather Mountain across the lake.

Walk through the parking lot, passing the Julian Price Park signboard, and enter the woods. You will soon enter Loop A of the campground. Walk along paved paths, and pass a bathroom and some campsites. At 2.1 miles, come to a fork with the Tanawha trailhead to the right. Turn left and continue back to the Boone Fork parking area.

2. Tanawha Trail

Round-trip: 5.4 miles
Hiking time: 3 hours
Best time to hike: Late spring, summer, and fall
High point: 4440 feet
Elevation gain: 275 feet
Difficulty: Strenuous
Rules and fees: Dogs must be on a leash no longer than 6 feet; to protect the fragile plant environment, dogs are not allowed on the section of the Tanawha Trail between Wilson Creek and Rough Ridge
Maps: USGS Grandfather Mountain; Blue Ridge Parkway Tanawha Trail
Contact: Blue Ridge Parkway headquarters, 828-271-4779; automated road and weather conditions, 828-298-0398; *www.nps.gov/blri*

Getting there: From Linville, take the Blue Ridge Parkway north about 12 miles to the Beacon Heights parking area, at milepost 305, on the right. (Just a mile farther north is the Linn Cove Visitor Center, which

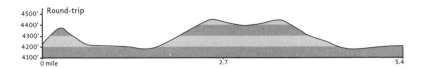

is open May through October and has trail maps, area guidebooks, and bathrooms.) Start the hike by crossing the dirt road and entering the woods by the sign that says, "Tanawha Trail Beacon Heights 0.2."

This is a rugged yet beautiful trail that will make your legs hurt while walking but will deliver a huge payoff—views to make your heart hurt. Take this hike on a clear, sunny day, preferably in fall—the perfect time of year.

The Tanawha (Cherokee for "great hawk") Trail stretches 13.5 miles, paralleling and crisscrossing the Blue Ridge Parkway from Beacon Heights at milepost 305 to the Price Lake Campground at milepost 297. To take in some of the trail's highlights, unless you are up for a marathon hike, try this 5.4-mile round-trip of the Tanawha from Beacon Heights to the Linn Cove Visitor Center, ending at Wilson Creek and then back. Start by taking a short, 0.6-mile round-trip on the Beacon Heights Trail for stunning views of Grandfather Mountain and other peaks along the Blue Ridge Parkway. There are steep drop-offs here, so be cautious with dogs.

Backtrack to the junction with the Tanawha Trail and turn right. Continue on rugged terrain—this is a hike for sure-footed and trail-hardy dogs—through dense forest of rhododendron, mountain laurel, spruce, and fir, while skirting large boulders and crossing boardwalks over particularly rough sections.

After hiking about 1.5 miles from the Tanawha trailhead, emerge from the woods onto a paved path that leads to the Linn Cove Visitor Center. The trail continues through the parking lot and under the Linn Cove Viaduct, a world-famous engineering feat that was built to bring motorists into the heart of the Grandfather Mountain terrain while still protecting its delicate plant life.

Climb some steps under the viaduct past rhododendrons, pines, and other evergreens. This is probably the roughest section of trail, where you will encounter otherworldly-type terrain—immense boulders tumbled together where you must navigate through narrow, rocky passages. It is a trail for people in good shape and for dogs with hardy, trail-traveled pads.

The trail levels out a bit as you walk through beautiful, huge, colorful leaves of oaks, tulip poplars, Fraser magnolias, beeches, and birches. At about 2.25 miles, come to a boulder field with natural springs running through the rocks that make good watering spots for dogs. At 2.5 miles, descend steep rock steps and come to a fork at a bridge over Wilson Creek. Rough Ridge—a high rock outcropping ringed with extremely fragile alpine plant life—is to the left, and to the right is Wilson Creek Overlook, a 0.1-mile walk up to the Blue Ridge Parkway. Stop here for a moment to enjoy the gentle cascades spilling down the rocks of Wilson Creek before turning

Angie and Sammy make their way through a boulder-strewn stretch of the Tanawha Trail.

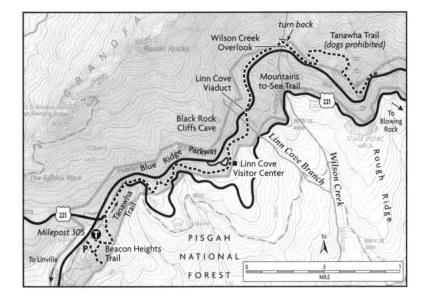

back. The Park Service instituted a ban on dogs from this part of the trail to Rough Ridge for fear of having them trample plants off trail.

If you are in a party with two vehicles, the Wilson Creek Overlook would be a good place to leave one vehicle for a shuttle. Otherwise, backtrack to the Beacon Heights parking area, or head back up to the overlook for a scenic lunch spot.

3. Crabtree Falls Loop Trail

Round-trip and loop: 2.5 miles
Hiking time: 1.5 to 2 hours
Best time to hike: Late spring, summer, and fall
High point: 3760 feet
Elevation gain: 530 feet
Difficulty: Moderate to strenuous
Rules and fees: Dogs must be on a leash no longer than 6 feet
Maps: USGS Celo; Blue Ridge Parkway Crabtree Falls Trail
Contact: Blue Ridge Parkway, 828-271-4779; automated road and
weather conditions, 828-298-0398; Spruce Pine Ranger Station
828-765-4319; *www.nps.gov/blri*

Getting there: From Spruce Pine, take the Blue Ridge Parkway south for about 8 miles to milepost 339. Turn right into the Crabtree Falls Campground and follow the signs to the Crabtree Falls trailhead parking area.

The picturesque Crabtree Falls Campground has an honor payment system for tent and RV camping, but there is no parking fee for day hiking. The campground and the Crabtree Falls Loop Trail are part of the popular, 250-acre Crabtree Meadows Recreation Area of the Blue Ridge Parkway, which also includes a picnic area, restaurant, and gift shop. The main attraction here is the waterfall. The best times of year to hike with dogs are late spring, summer, and fall. The parkway at this high elevation is intermittently closed during winter due to snowy or icy road conditions, and the road to the campground is closed from the end of October through May. If the parkway is open you can still access the trail in the off-season by parking at the gate and walking 0.3 mile from the parkway to the trailhead.

Start the hike at the trailhead sign, bearing right. Enter a dense forest of hemlock, rhododendron, maple, hickory, and other hardwoods. The trail descends quickly, down a series of wooden stairs set into the ground. Arrive at a trail intersection near a wooden bench at 0.2 mile. Take the right fork, which leads to the falls in 0.7 mile.

The area is very lush, and it seems that vegetation grows bigger here—at most points along the trail the oversize oak, maple, and tulip poplar leaves form a tight-knit, leafy roof, keeping the trail cool and shaded in summer. In spring you'll find a profusion of colorful wildflowers, such as trillium, violet, buttercup, and jack-in-the-pulpit, as well as blooming rhododendron and mountain laurel. The trail edges are thickly lined with shrubby plants, ferns, and waxy-leafed galax. The trail itself gets very rocky, so watch your footing and your dog's paws—this might be a difficult trail for dogs with sensitive pads.

At about 0.4 mile you will start to hear the rush of the falls. The trail can be wet and muddy, as well as rocky, through here, so be sure to wear sturdy hiking boots with ankle support. At 0.5 mile two more sets

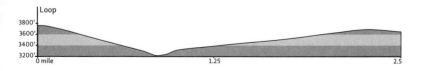

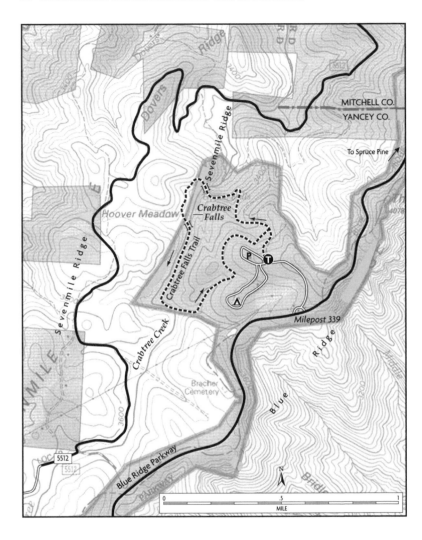

of stone stairs lead to a series of switchbacks. Cross a small footbridge, and then descend two more sets of stone steps. Continue on a fairly rocky trail until the falls finally appear out of the dense forest at the 0.9-mile point.

The 60-foot-high Crabtree Falls plunge and tumble over rocky ledges into a deep, cold pool, offering a welcome break for dogs who want to cool their paws and take a drink. However, with large, uneven, and slippery rocks to negotiate, reaching the pool can be tricky.

Crabtree Falls is a cool, refreshing destination halfway around the Crabtree Falls Loop Trail.

Directly in front of the falls is a sturdy wooden bridge across Crabtree Creek, with a bench for relaxing and picture taking. The beauty of the gushing falls can be mesmerizing, and you will want to linger here—along with many other people and dogs. Crabtree Falls is a very popular hike, especially in summer and during the fall foliage season. Try the hike in early spring or on a weekday or early morning, when the trail is usually less crowded.

To return to the trailhead, cross the bridge to continue on the loop trail. Be forewarned—this is where you and the pooch will get a workout and pay for the privilege of viewing the pretty falls.

Immediately after the bridge, start some serious climbing up a set of stone steps. The trail is very narrow here and is sometimes slippery with water and mud. Ascend on switchbacks and another set of stone stairs, and soon you will walk through a thick mountain laurel tunnel.

After you hear the rush of falls on the left, you will soon see a small cascade where dogs will want to take a side trip for a drink after the hard climb. At about 0.5 mile after leaving Crabtree Falls, you will come to a bridge, where there is easy access for dogs to get water. The trail levels off and continues, parallel to the creek.

At 2 miles you will pass by a bench, and shortly after you will come to an intersection with a sign for campground Loop B to the right. Turn left here to continue the loop trail. At the next intersection, turn right and ascend the set of stairs that heads back to the parking area.

4. Old Mitchell Trail

Loop: 4.4 miles
Hiking time: 3 hours
Best time to hike: Late spring, summer, and fall
High point: 6684 feet
Elevation gain: 580 feet
Difficulty: Strenuous
Rules and fees: Dogs must be on a leash no longer than 6 feet
Maps: USGS Mount Mitchell; Mount Mitchell State Park
Contact: Mount Mitchell State Park, 828-675-4611, *www.ncparks.gov;*
automated road and weather conditions, 828-298-0398

Getting there: From Asheville, take the Blue Ridge Parkway north about 30 miles to milepost 355. Turn left onto NC 128 at the sign for Mount Mitchell State Park. If traveling from Interstate 40 east of Asheville, take exit 86/NC 226 to Marion/Shelby. NC 226 merges with US 221 and US 70 in Marion. Veer left on US 70. After another 2 miles, turn north on NC 80, follow it for 16 miles, and then turn left onto the Blue Ridge Parkway. At milepost 355 turn right onto NC 128. Drive 2 miles to the park office and park there to start the Old Mitchell Trail.

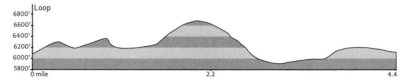

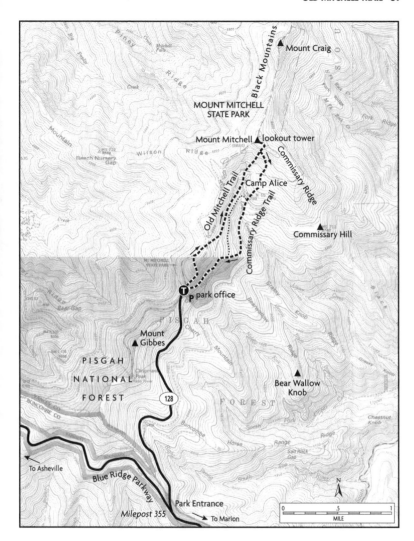

Mount Mitchell is a hike that dogs with sure footing and long, heavy coats will love. The state park is named for its prominent summit—Mount Mitchell—which is also the highest peak in the eastern United States, at 6684 feet elevation. The entire park, including numerous hiking trails, a campground, picnic area, restaurant, and museum, sits above 6000 feet, keeping it cool throughout summer and usually closed in winter due to severe weather, strong winds, and snowy, icy roads. Its alpine environment more closely resembles the climate of Canada than the surrounding Southern Appalachians.

Glenn and Shelby arrive at the highest mountain peak in the eastern United States—Mount Mitchell.

This loop is a great hike for dogs as it combines the Old Mitchell, Camp Alice, and Commissary Ridge Trails. Start at the Old Mitchell trailhead in front of the park office. Immediately enter a spruce–fir forest and follow a yellow circle blaze to start climbing a trail softly padded with rich soil and fallen evergreen needles. At 0.1 mile, the trail opens up and out of the forest to many dead trees—the unfortunate victims of air pollution, acid precipitation, and the balsam woolly adelgid, an exotic insect pest that has been killing the Fraser firs since the 1950s.

The bare trees are intermingled with healthier new growth, including maple, birch, mountain ash, and red spruce. In spring and summer, ferns, daisies, bluets, St. John's wort, and other wildflowers line the trail's edges. At 0.5 mile the trail emerges to an unusual sight in the woods—a restaurant sitting in a mowed field. Dogs are not allowed inside, so walk straight ahead on a paved path to the parking area. Turn right and follow the yellow blazes.

Continue climbing and descending through hemlock, fir, and spruce. Intermittent—and stunning—views can be enjoyed through the trees. Hike on a clear day to get the most of the vistas. At 0.95 mile arrive at a bridge that passes over steep, wet rocks, and you will soon come to steep wood stairs. The high rainfall and heavy tree cover keep the trail conditions slick. Wear sturdy boots, make sure dogs are able to handle the terrain, and bring plenty of water for them—you will find no suitable drinking sources.

At 1.35 miles arrive at an intersection with the Camp Alice Trail, blazed in blue squares. (You will take this trail on the return). For now, turn left, following the yellow blazes. At 1.5 miles and about 6400 feet elevation, the climbing really starts—you can see the summit rising through the trees. Another 0.3 mile brings you to an intersection. Turn right, and at 1.75 miles emerge from the woods onto a gravel road.

To reach the summit observation platform (which replaced a stone tower and is scheduled to open in fall 2007), turn right and walk 0.2 mile up a paved path. Pass the gravesite of Elisha Mitchell—a University of North Carolina professor who is credited with measuring the peak in 1844, and for whom it is named. The observation deck offers 360-degree views of the Black Mountains and the Blue Ridge Mountains.

Backtrack to the Old Mitchell trailhead for the return loop. Restrooms, museum, gift shop, and concession stand are farther down the road, but dogs are not allowed in the buildings. Head back on the Old Mitchell Trail until it forks with the Camp Alice Trail. Take this trail, following the blue blazes.

Begin a steep descent over wet rocks. After about 1 mile, descend stone stairs to an intersection with the Commissary Ridge Trail. This is the site of Camp Alice, where visitors in the early twentieth century stayed during visits to the Black Mountains. Turn right here onto an old gravel road, and follow the orange diamonds for about 1 mile back to the park office parking area. From here, it's a fairly level walk, although the gravel can irritate the padding on some dogs' feet. The change in terrain and the open views are a refreshing way to end the hike, arriving back at the park office.

5. Big Butt Trail

Round-trip: 6 miles

Hiking time: 4 hours

Best time to hike: Spring through fall

High point: 5900 feet

Elevation gain: 600 feet

Difficulty: Strenuous

Rules and fees: Dogs must be on a leash on Blue Ridge Parkway
  property, and on U.S. Forest Service land and state game land
  between April 1 and August 15

Map: USGS Mount Mitchell

Contact: Blue Ridge Parkway headquarters, 828-271-4779; automated
  road and weather conditions, 828-298-0398; *www.nps.gov/blri*

Getting there: Traveling north from the Asheville area, take the Blue
Ridge Parkway to milepost 359 at the Balsam Gap pullout on the left. It
is about 25 miles northeast of Asheville and 4 miles south of the turnoff
to Mount Mitchell State Park.

Once you get past the name of the trail, you and your dog will thoroughly
enjoy this lovely, remote hike. Some steep, strenuous climbing sections
mean you should make sure the pooch is fit and up for the challenge. Also
bring plenty of water because you will find no reliable streams or springs
along the way. This trail is best hiked from spring through fall; winter is
uncomfortably cold at this altitude and is often inaccessible because the
Blue Ridge Parkway is frequently closed then. The trail is at its prettiest
in spring, starting in mid-April when it is bursting with wildflowers.

Start at the Balsam Gap pullout on the parkway at an elevation of
5320 feet and start the trail at the south end of the parking area. The Big
Butt Trail is blazed with a white rectangle—the nearby Mountains-to-Sea
Trail is blazed with a white circle. Descend into an evergreen forest and
a sea of wildflowers, including trillium, violet, bluet, and mayapple. The

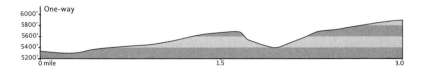

This view from Little Butt, on the Big Butt Trail, is one of the hike's highlights.

ground, completely carpeted in flowers, looks white, pink, and purple rather than brown and green.

Keep winding and climbing through an evergreen forest, stepping over many tree roots and gliding through a sea of wildflowers. The trail leaves Park Service property a few minutes into the hike and passes into the Pisgah National Forest and North Carolina Game Lands, where hunting is allowed in season, generally November through April. Putting a hunter orange vest on your dog (as well as the people on the hike) during those times is advisable.

At 0.4 mile enter an area dense with rhododendron, rocky footing, and a lot of downed trees on the sides of the trail. Soon you are walking along Brush Fence Ridge. In spring and summer, when the weather is warm and the flowers are abundant, this trail is not frequently traveled, so you can often find solitude, even on weekends.

At 1.6 miles, you will arrive at Point Misery at 5715 feet elevation. You will understand the name a little better on the return, since the climb is steep. From here, descend rapidly on a muddy, rocky path riddled with tree roots and switchbacks, heading in a northwesterly direction.

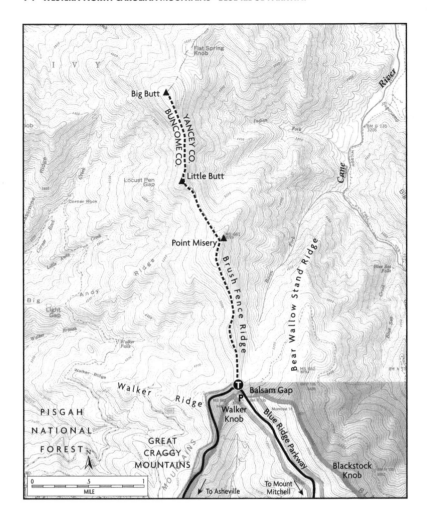

Keep descending, dropping down into a hardwood forest and, from April to June, passing through fields dotted with red-flowered trillium, also known as wake robin. At times it feels as if you are traipsing through someone's perfectly unkempt flower garden—there are so many blooms. At just over 2 miles begin a very steep ascent, where in some places you will have to use your hands to hoist yourself up. Older or overweight dogs or those with short legs might have trouble here. Enter a rhododendron and mountain laurel–framed trail with beautiful views spread left of the narrow trail as it hugs the ledge.

Dogs with their noses to the ground will no doubt sniff out a slightly less trampled spur trail that veers off to the right at about 2.3 miles at Little Butt. It leads to a rock ledge that provides perfect seating to witness a perfect, sweeping view of the Black Mountains to the east. Hold on tightly to dogs if they are prone to wandering—the drop-offs are steep and sudden.

This is a good spot for a rest and a drink after the arduous climb. A backtrack from here will make for a nearly 5-mile round-trip hike. Or, continue on the main trail for nearly a mile more to Big Butt. You can see the destination ahead as the trail starts to narrow and become overgrown with dense, thorny underbrush, almost to the point of bushwhacking in places. You are walking along a ridge, and when the vegetation thins out in places, there are long-ranging views on either side of the trail. The actual Big Butt summit is hard to access due to the thick, overgrown vegetation, but you should arrive there at about 3 miles. Retrace your steps to the trailhead.

6. Craggy Pinnacle Trail

Round-trip: 1.4 miles

Hiking time: 1 hour

Best time to hike: Mid to late June for rhododendron bloom, summer, and fall

High point: 5892 feet

Elevation gain: 250 feet

Difficulty: Moderate

Rules and fees: Dogs must be on a leash no longer than 6 feet

Map: USGS Craggy Pinnacle

Contact: Blue Ridge Parkway headquarters, 828-271-4779; automated road and weather conditions, 828-298-0398; *www.nps.gov/blri*

Getting there: From Asheville, take the Blue Ridge Parkway north about 18 miles to milepost 364. You will see the Craggy Gardens Visitor Center on the left. Continue past the visitor center and go through the Craggy Pinnacle Tunnel. Just after the tunnel, the parking area for the Craggy Pinnacle trailhead is on the left.

The best time of year to hike in the Craggy Gardens area is mid to late June, simply for the magnificent show of the pinkish-purple Catawba

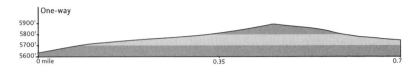

rhododendron blooms. But the scenic views from the summit of Craggy Pinnacle make this a worthy hike any time of year that the Blue Ridge Parkway is accessible to this point. Due to the high elevation (close to 5900 feet), the winter months can bring hazardous driving conditions with snow, ice, and slick roads, forcing the Park Service to close off access. Always call the parkway's automated road and weather condition phone number before heading out. The Craggy Gardens Visitor Center has bathrooms, a ranger or salesperson on duty, and maps and books for sale, but it has no phone and is open only from May through October.

Start the trail at an interpretive sign that tells the story of the Catawba rhododendron, named for the Catawba Indians who lived east of the Catawba River. These evergreen trees are known as "nature's thermometer" since their leaves curl inward when the temperature drops below 35°F. When the temperature drops into the teens, leaves turn brownish and curl so tightly they resemble string beans.

Head onto the trail, which starts off in a thick tunnel of rhododendron that hugs the trail most of the way. The trail is wide, slightly rocky, and steep, but well traveled through the season. Dogs must be on a leash at all times. At 0.2 mile, come to a large rock outcropping on the left and an overlook on the right, then soon to a bench on the right and a fork in the trail. A sign indicates access to the lower overlook on the right, and the summit overlook to the left. Take the right fork to descend a few hundred feet to a stone wall with views of the Blue Ridge Parkway and the visitor center below. Signs warn hikers to stay on trail to avoid damaging the delicate plant life that abounds here. Make sure your dogs stay on trail as well. Backtrack to the intersection and take the summit trail.

At just under 0.5 mile from the trailhead is the Craggy Pinnacle summit at 5892 feet elevation. If the day is clear and it is not too windy, the overlook is the perfect perch for sitting awhile on one of the benches or the circular stone wall and taking in the 360-degree view of the Blue Ridge Mountains, the parkway, and the reservoir that provides drinking water for the city of Asheville, about 20 miles to the southwest.

More interpretive signs at the summit detail the rare plants that grow in the cracks of rocks, such as foamflower, which is usually found in Canadian alpine environments, and three-toothed cinquefoil. These plants, along with blueberry bushes and other shrubbery in the heath family, can be seen without stepping over the wall. At the peak of the Catawba rhododendron bloom, this is also a great place to see the mountainsides speckled in pink. Head back to the parking area the way you came.

For another nearby leg stretcher, drive back to the visitor center and take the Craggy Gardens Nature Trail at the southern end of the parking area. It leads about 1 mile through a thick covering of rhododendron,

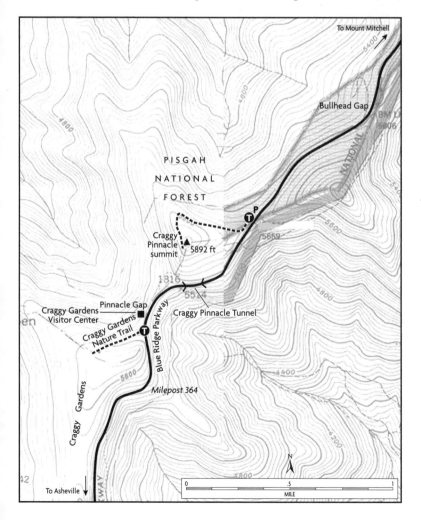

Holly and Elliot make their way down a rhododendron tunnel on the Craggy Pinnacle Trail with Wesley, a bichon frisé-poodle mix.

passes a picnic shelter built in the 1930s by the Civilian Conservation Corps, and emerges from the woods at the Craggy Gardens Picnic Area. The colorful blooms, as well as some blueberries in August, make this a nice hike, although the more sweeping, scenic views are best seen from the top of the pinnacle.

7. Snowball Trail

Round-trip: 6 miles
Hiking time: 4 hours
Best time to hike: Late spring, summer, and fall
High point: 5330 feet
Elevation gain: 1000 feet
Difficulty: Strenuous
Rules and fees: Dogs must be on a leash on Blue Ridge Parkway property, and under control on U.S. Forest Service and North Carolina Game Lands property
Map: USGS Craggy Pinnacle
Contact: Blue Ridge Parkway headquarters, 828-271-4779; automated road and weather conditions, 828-298-0398; *www.nps.gov/blri*

Getting there: Traveling from Asheville, take the Blue Ridge Parkway north about 20 miles. Turn left into the Craggy Gardens Picnic Area at milepost 367.7 and drive about 0.5 mile. Park on the left by Forest Service Road 63, being careful not to block the gated road. Start the hike at the Mountains-to-Sea Trail sign.

During spring and summer, you are more likely to find a giant white pine, a sudden and stunning mountain view, or a burst of colorful wildflowers than you are to find a snowball on this hike. But at this high elevation, in late fall or winter, balls of snow are very possible. The trail also makes a good hike in the colder months when all the thick leaves have fallen

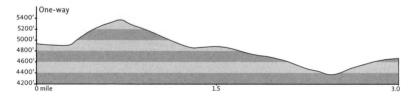

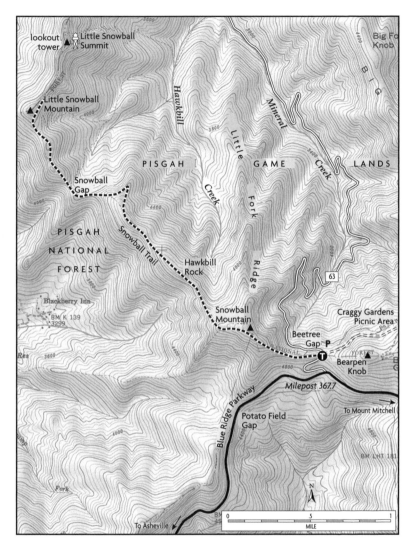

and mountain views appear as you walk across the ridgeline. However, the Blue Ridge Parkway is often closed to vehicle traffic during winter, so this trail is usually not accessible then.

The Snowball is a deep-woods trail easily accessible off the Blue Ridge Parkway. It is off-limits to bicycles and horses and is even little used by hikers, so it is perfect for dogs. But there are strenuous climbs, so make sure your dog is tough, trail-hardy, and ready for a workout.

The trailhead is near the scenic Craggy Gardens Picnic Area, and you can pack a lunch to enjoy there after the hike. The trail has rock outcrops and fallen tree trunks that serve as perfect picnic spots as well.

Start at the Mountains-to-Sea trailhead sign just to the left of gated Forest Service Road 63. Start climbing and come to a fork at 0.1 mile. The white-blazed Mountains-to-Sea Trail goes left. Take the Snowball Trail, blazed with a yellow rectangle, which veers to the right.

Mary and her daughter, Carson, take a break with their border collie, Maddie, on a rock overlook on the Snowball Trail.

The narrow trail surface is hard-packed earth and mud that leads you through a dense forest of mountain ash blooming with bright red berries in early September, along with buckeye, beech, birch, and other hardwoods that make this a very colorful fall hike. In 0.25 mile ascend the stairs on your left to switchbacks. In spring through early fall, pass through a walkway sprayed with colorful wildflowers and leafy ferns, plenty to keep dogs' noses busy.

The trail continues to climb relentlessly, gaining more than 300 feet in elevation in the stretch of a half mile, until you arrive at 0.7 mile at the top of Snowball Mountain, sometimes called Big Snowball. This peak sits at the southern end of Little Fork Ridge.

In late fall and winter, you'll have views from both sides of the ridgeline. Footing can be slippery in these months, with the many dry leaves covering the ground, so be careful. Descend from the peak. At 0.9 mile some switchbacks lead through a variety of oak, beech, birch, maple, locust, spruce, and other evergreen trees. In just over 1 mile, come up onto a ridge with mountain views on both sides and the summit of Little Snowball visible to the northeast. You are walking through oak, maple, rhododendron, and other shrubbery, with large patches of the skunky-smelling, evergreen galax plant, which dogs will enjoy sniffing out.

At about 1.3 miles start a steep scramble up to Hawkbill Rock at 4800 feet elevation. A large rock slab to the left offers beautiful, rolling mountain views to the northwest and into the Reems Creek area. Many hikers make this their destination for enjoying a picnic on a clear day.

If the dogs have more energy to burn, continue on the trail. Start scrambling up steep, large, sometimes slippery boulders, which you will have to climb using hands. Small dogs will almost certainly need to be lifted here and larger dogs might need a boost. This section is only for the surest-footed dogs with good leg strength and flexibility.

The trail continues to undulate, dipping and climbing, but stays on the ridgeline. Avoid taking any of the trails that branch off to the right and left—this way you will stay on the Snowball Trail, which is not well blazed. Since the trail passes through the Pisgah Game Lands, which is national forest land where hunting is permitted in season, it is advisable to wear blaze orange clothing and have dogs wear a blaze orange vest during fall and winter.

At about 2 miles start dropping down more steeply and enter a long stand of tall maples at Snowball Gap. At 2.3 miles, come to a fork in a clearing area and turn left. Keep ascending, often having to climb over or walk around large trees that have fallen across the trail. At the next fork, at about 2.6 miles, continue straight up to Little Snowball and the remains of an old fire tower, before backtracking.

8. Rattlesnake Lodge Trail

Round-trip: 3.2 miles
Hiking time: 2 hours
Best time to hike: Spring through late fall
High point: 3800 feet
Elevation gain: 650 feet
Difficulty: Moderate to strenuous
Rules and fees: Dogs must be on a leash no longer than 6 feet
Map: USGS Craggy Pinnacle
Contact: Blue Ridge Parkway, 828-271-4779; automated road and
    weather conditions, 828-298-0398; *www.nps.gov/blri;* Friends of
    the Mountains-to-Sea Trail, 919-496-4771; *www.ncmst.org*

Getting there: From Asheville, take the Blue Ridge Parkway north for about 7 miles and turn left at Bull Gap, just past milepost 376 on the parkway. Drive 0.3 mile to the intersection with Elk Mountain Scenic Highway and bear right. Drive 0.5 mile and pull off at the dirt parking area on the right (the second parking area you come to). Head up the trail and turn left onto the Mountains-to-Sea Trail, which is blazed with a white circle.

This is one of those hikes that holds natural and man-made wonders, making it a special hike for both dogs and their people. The trail is named for the actual Rattlesnake Lodge, which sat tucked away in this hidden mountaintop retreat for about twenty years in the early 1900s. The stone remains of the lodge await at the end of the trail, a treat for history buffs

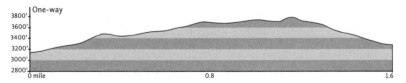

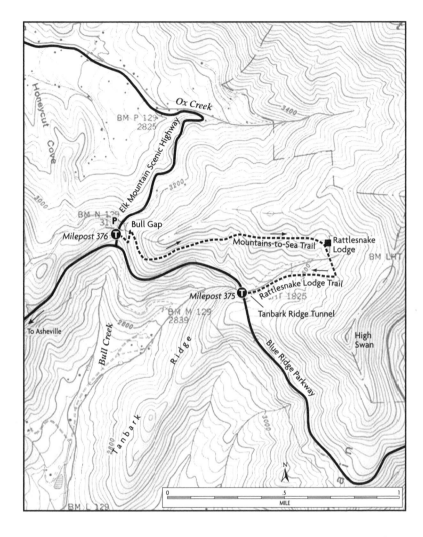

and anyone with a sense of curiosity. The lodge can be accessed from two separate trailheads. Decide at the outset if you (and your dog) prefer a slow and steady ascent or a fast and strenuous one.

The slow and winding route begins at Bull Gap. It starts with some slowly ascending switchbacks on a narrow, rocky path following the Mountains-to-Sea Trail through a hardwood forest. The winter and early spring seasons offer great views of the surrounding mountains and valleys while there are no leaves on the trees. Mid-spring brings out a multitude of trailside wildflowers, including the white-colored bloodroot, violets, large-flowered trillium, and the bright-red flowers known as fire pink. The trail is also lined with rhododendron and mountain laurel, whose flowers bloom in May and June. The switchbacks only last about 0.2 mile, and then the trail winds around large boulders and hugs cliff sides, with deep valleys below.

About 1 mile into the trail, arrive at a large stone foundation on the right, then farther down is a circular stone foundation—a former swimming pool. A National Park Service interpretive sign nearby tells the history of Rattlesnake Lodge, the summer home of Dr. Chase P. Ambler, a prominent Asheville physician, his wife, and their five children. The

Flame azalea is one of the many colorful blooms that make the Rattlesnake Lodge Trail a nice early spring hike.

family lived in the sprawling, hidden retreat in the early 1900s. The two-story lodge was built from hand-hewn chestnut, and all the home's furniture was built from timber felled on the property. Items that could not be built on site were brought in on horseback.

The lodge was quite a marvel for its day and its location—it had indoor bathrooms, heated running water, even electricity produced from a small generator. The "estate" contained several outbuildings, a tennis court and pool, and a working farm.

Ambler wrote an article about the lodge for *Forest and Stream* magazine in May 1906. "Here was a house site, at an elevation sufficient to insure coolness in summer; abundant water of the finest quality; a site well sheltered from storms by the wall or ridge on three sides; a nook while not giving the extended views in all direction that can be had from many nearby points, yet was secure from storm," he wrote of the site's spectacular, secluded location.

The family sold the lodge in 1920, the same year that Dr. Ambler became chair of a committee that formed the southern chapter of the Appalachian Mountain Club. The lodge burned in 1926, most likely from a lightning strike, and the property was acquired by the Park Service in 1976.

After marveling at the past, pass by the springhouse remains, where cool water still trickles, watering perennials planted a century before, and continue on the Mountains-to-Sea Trail. Cross a small stream and arrive at a chimney foundation from the old tenants' shack, which the Amblers provided for hikers passing through. Here, the steeper, 0.4-mile trail descends on a blue-blazed trail to the Blue Ridge Parkway. Either backtrack from here to Bull Gap, or head downhill on the Rattlesnake Lodge Trail and the parkway. Walking along the parkway with a dog is not recommended, so return the way you came.

If you decide to head down the steep Rattlesnake Lodge Trail, about three-fourths of the way down this trail you will come to a stream where the dogs can cool their paws and take a drink. Because of the steepness of the trail and the propensity to linger on top, be sure to bring drinking water for yourself and your dog.

If you want to hike just the 0.4-mile Rattlesnake Lodge Trail (named for the abundance of rattlers the Ambler family found on the property), start at milepost 375, parking just south of the Tanbark Ridge Tunnel. Park on either side of the parkway, and start the trail by the stream on the west side of the parkway. A good workout is to start here, climb to the lodge, hike to Bull Gap, and then return.

9. Mount Pisgah and Buck Spring Lodge Trails

Round-trip: 2.4 miles
Hiking time: 1.5 hours
Best time to hike: Year-round, Blue Ridge Parkway road conditions permitting
High point: 5721 feet
Elevation gain: 712 feet
Difficulty: Strenuous
Rules and fees: Dogs must be on a 6-foot leash
Maps: USGS Dunsmore Mountain; USGS Cruso
Contact: Blue Ridge Parkway, 828-271-4779; automated road and weather conditions, 828-298-0398; *www.nps.gov/blri*

Getting there: From Asheville, take the Blue Ridge Parkway south about 20 miles to the Mount Pisgah area. Turn left at milepost 407 at the Mount Pisgah parking sign (before getting to the Pisgah Inn). Go up the road 0.2 mile to the second parking area, where it dead ends at the trailhead. During the weekends of the busier seasons—summer and fall—you might need to park in the first parking area, or even continue farther south on the parkway to a large parking area on the right, and walk back to the trailhead.

The Mount Pisgah Trail is all about climbing, so it is only suitable for the most trail-hardy dogs (and people), but it is worth the effort for everyone involved. After all, the peak is named for the biblical mountain from which Moses is said to have seen the Promised Land. The views from the summit of Mount Pisgah—one of the highest and most recognizable in the Blue Ridge range—just might rival the ones Moses saw.

Start on the trail at an already hefty altitude of 5009 feet. If you are recently coming from sea level, your breathing might be heavier than

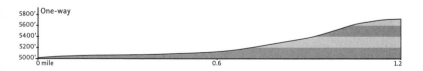

usual on this hike. A couple of tiny streams run near the trail, but they are not a reliable drinking source for dogs, so be sure to bring plenty of water and extra snacks.

The trail starts out wide and level, but at just over 0.3 mile, it will start to narrow and rise sharply. It also becomes rocky in places, so periodically you should check your dog's paws if he or she tends to have sensitive pads.

This is a great hike in early fall because the leaves on hardwood trees are changing color (and no hunting is allowed on National Park Service

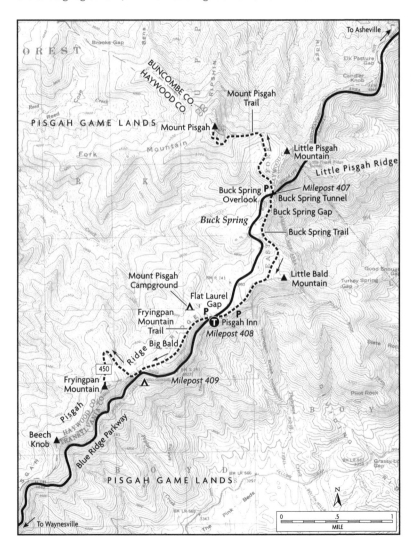

The summit of Mount Pisgah juts up out of the Pisgah National Forest, as seen from the parking area below.

land) and in summer because the heavy leaf cover of oak, beech, and birch provides shade from the sun. But late winter and spring are also nice, and actually preferable, because the views are wide open and the cooler air provides a more comfortable hiking atmosphere for people and dogs.

The trail heads in a northwesterly direction, lined thickly with rhododendron. To the west are wide views of the Pisgah National Forest, and to the northwest you can make out the destination—Mount Pisgah, easily identifiable by the television tower that juts up from its summit. The trail continues climbing in front of you. It is a much-loved and well-used trail, so at any time of year you are sure to encounter many other users, especially on weekends. Step to the right when approaching other hikers, allowing downhill and dogless hikers the right-of-way.

At about 0.9 mile, the trail turns sharply northeast, with a perfect view off to the west of the rolling Balsam Mountains. Large stone steps here assist with the climbing, which becomes even steeper and more shrouded by rhododendron on the last, narrow, rocky push to the summit. The rather ugly and garish TV tower might be the first thing you see when topping out on Mount Pisgah, but climb up onto the wooden observation platform from where you will get long, sweeping views. To the south you can see the Blue Ridge Parkway and the Pisgah Inn (a motel, restaurant, and gift shop a mile south on the parkway; the inn does not allow dogs).

The observation deck is a nice place to catch your breath, give the dogs some water from their collapsible drinking bowls, and take great pictures. At close to 6000 feet in elevation, the summit is often much cooler and windier than at the trailhead. Wearing layers, especially a wind- and water-repellent jacket, is a wise way to go. After enjoying the view, retrace your steps to the trailhead, being careful as you descend the steep trail, since rocks are often slick with runoff.

Heading out of the parking lot, you come to Buck Spring Overlook on the left, with more opportunities for panoramic views. To the right of this overlook is a sign leading to another overlook and the Mount Pisgah "Lodge" 1 mile away, which is a nice and easy side trip to the Pisgah Inn. Climb some stairs, and after 500 feet the trail comes to the remains of Buck Spring Lodge. This was George Washington Vanderbilt's hunting lodge. The buildings were removed in 1963, but you can admire the views from some benches.

Vanderbilt was the grandson of Cornelius "Commodore" Vanderbilt of New York, who amassed a millionaire's fortune in the 1800s in the shipping and railroad industries. George Vanderbilt made a name for himself in the Asheville area by creating an enormous estate on the banks of the French Broad River and building the French château–style Biltmore House in 1895, which remains the largest private residence in the United States. The house, part of the Biltmore Estate, along with a winery, gardens, and activities such as horseback riding and fly-fishing, is operated now as a tourist attraction in Asheville.

10. Fryingpan Mountain Trail

Round-trip: 4 miles
Hiking time: 2 hours
Best time to hike: Year-round, Blue Ridge Parkway road conditions
   permitting
High point: 5280 feet
Elevation gain: 340 feet
Difficulty: Moderate
Rules and fees: Dogs must be on a leash on Blue Ridge Parkway
   property, but not on the U.S. Forest Service roads
Maps: USGS Cruso; Blue Ridge Parkway Mount Pisgah Trails
Contact: Blue Ridge Parkway headquarters, 828-271-4779; automated
   road and weather conditions, 828-298-0398; *www.nps.gov/blri*

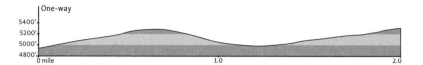

Getting there: Traveling from Asheville, take the Blue Ridge Parkway south about 30 miles to the Mount Pisgah Campground at milepost 408, just south of the Pisgah Inn. Turn right into the campground and park on the left, adjacent to the Fryingpan Mountain Trail sign.

If you happen to be camping in one of the loveliest spots on the Blue Ridge Parkway—the Mount Pisgah Campground—then this hike is a must-do for you and the dogs. Even if you are just out for a day drive, you should check out this trail.

The hike starts right at the campground entrance but, strangely, only attracts moderate use. Most visitors head down the road to the better known and hugely popular Mount Pisgah Trail. Although no biblically named mountaintop peak awaits on this trail, it is a wonderful walk in the woods to another summit area with great views.

Spring, summer, and fall are all nice times of year to explore Fryingpan Mountain because of the abundance of wildflowers that grow along the trail edges. Winter can also be a good time to hike because the fallen leaves open up sweeping views as you walk along the ridgeline, but often in winter the parkway at this elevation is closed to motor traffic.

Park at the entrance to the campground, across from the ranger kiosk, alongside the Fryingpan Mountain Trail sign. Start climbing gradually on a narrow trail that alternates between rocks and roots and well-packed earth and grass. Dogs will find lots of vegetation to sniff on all sides. Walk through a Park Service maintenance area with picnic tables, and continue on the trail lined with azalea, mountain laurel, and dogwood sporting big white blooms in spring. In late summer and early fall, goldenrod abounds, as well as yellow aster and a sweeping sea of white snakeroot bushes. Due to the high altitude here—the trail starts at close to 5000 feet elevation—leaves also start to change color earlier in fall.

At just under 0.5 mile you come onto the 5180-foot-high ridgeline of Big Bald with views out across the parkway to the rippling mountains. Overhead are oaks with their great, broad branches bending over the trail. Pass by large clusters of ferns at your feet and maples and mountain ash trees looming over the trail. Soon you start to descend into Fryingpan Gap.

Shelby walks through a sea of snakeroot and other wildflowers on the Fryingpan Mountain Trail in spring.

After 1 mile from the trailhead, arrive at gravel Forest Service Road 450. To the left, beyond a gate, is milepost 409.6 on the Blue Ridge Parkway. Turn right here and head up the road, which leads to the summit of Fryingpan Mountain and a fire tower. Since this is now U.S. Forest Service property, if your dog will stick by you it is okay to let her off the leash here.

This road is beautifully lined with colorful, pungent wildflowers from May through September, so it's a treat both for people to look at and for dogs to sniff. However, the road can be rocky and rough on softly padded feet. If you are on a long drive down the parkway and only have a short time for a walk, you can drive to the gate on the parkway and just do this 2-mile round-trip to the summit and back—a good leg stretcher.

The road continues to climb gradually and wind around bends with occasional views of the mountains and an abundance of wildflowers, such as thin-leaved sunflower, black-eyed Susan, and the purplish hollow joe-pye weed, in late summer and early fall.

At just about 2 miles from the trailhead, arrive at the top of Fryingpan Mountain. The immediate surroundings are not the prettiest—powerlines, a rusty fire tower, and outbuildings dot the landscape—but the surrounding views are awesome. Mount Pisgah looms to the northeast, easily recognizable by the TV tower jutting from its pointy, 5721-foot summit, and majestic, 6030-foot-high Cold Mountain appears to the west.

Dogs are not allowed to climb the fire tower steps, but you can enjoy the view from the ground before backtracking to the Mount Pisgah Campground.

11. Graveyard Fields Trail

Loop: 3.4 miles
Hiking time: 2 hours
Best time to hike: Spring through fall
High point: 5280 feet
Elevation gain: 300 feet
Difficulty: Moderate
Rules and fees: Dogs must be on a 6-foot leash on National Park
Service property
Map: USGS Shining Rock
Contact: Blue Ridge Parkway, 828-271-4779; automated road and
weather conditions, 828-298-0398; Pisgah Ranger District, Pisgah
National Forest, 828-877-3265; *www.cs.unca.edu/nfsnc*

Getting there: From the Asheville area, take the Blue Ridge Parkway
about 35 miles south to milepost 418, which is about 9 miles south of
the Pisgah Inn. The parking area for Graveyard Fields is on the right.

Its gruesome name notwithstanding, Graveyard Fields is an enormously
popular and much beloved trail. The area was named for devastating
forest fires that swept through in 1925, burning 25,000 acres, and in
1942, burning an equal amount, leaving the high-elevation valley with
blackened tree stumps that looked like tombstones.

The name has not kept hikers away—the area is so popular that parking
at the small pullout fills to overflowing on weekends, especially during
summer and fall. This is a must-do hike, but consider hitting the trail in
the off-season or during the week to avoid high foot traffic.

The popularity both for hikers and their dogs is understandable.
Graveyard Fields boasts a well-marked, easy-to-follow trail, two waterfalls,
riverside viewing, blueberry picking in late summer, and, at this high
elevation, cool temperatures throughout the summer.

Start the trail by descending the stairs at the northern end of the
parking area. The stairs and the paved path descend steeply into a

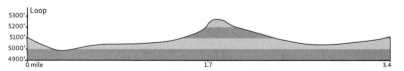

rhododendron and mountain laurel tunnel lined with trillium and galax. At 0.2 mile, the pavement turns to dirt, and often mud, in this high-rainfall environment and steeply descends over slippery rocks to a footbridge across Yellowstone Prong. Dogs will no doubt want to stop here for a cool drink. People will want to drink in the view, especially in fall, when the river carves over stones and splashes through the autumn-colored leaves, offering scenery that is spectacular.

Cross the bridge and bear right following the blue blaze to Lower Yellowstone Falls.

Turn right at the next trailhead sign, following the path for another 0.2 mile to a set of wooden stairs and some precariously steep and rocky footing to the base of the falls, at an elevation just under 5000 feet. Make sure dogs are fit enough for the climb back to the top. There is a small but cold and clear pool at the bottom of the falls where dogs can swim.

After enjoying the roaring falls and the splash time, backtrack to the trail junction and turn right, following the trail to Upper Yellowstone Falls. Pass through fields of blueberry bushes that ripen in late July

The popular Graveyard Fields area takes its name from the wind-thrown and burned tree trunks that appeared to look like tombstones.

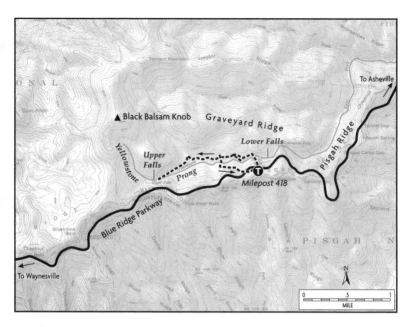

through August, a time when many people come to camp along the river. At 0.7 mile a trail sign points to a stream access to the left. Continue on the main trail to Upper Yellowstone Falls, bearing right at the sign and taking a left at the next intersection (which, turning right, leads to the Graveyard Ridge Trail). Pass through forests of spruce, fir, pine, birch, oak, and dogwood. Marvel at the high, rugged mountains that completely surround the little river valley.

Slowly start to climb in elevation as you continue on the narrow path, stepping over rocks and roots and crossing the stream several times. In some places boardwalks prevent further erosion to the trail. At 1.8 miles, after a steep and strenuous climb, you will come to the first overlook of Upper Yellowstone Falls. The large boulders just below the falls make great picnic spots while you gaze at the falls above, although these are not as impressive as Lower Yellowstone Falls. A short trail continues farther up to the top of the falls, but you'll not find a secure place to view them with your canine friend since it is easy for dogs to slide down the steep, slippery rocks of the falls; thus, your dog should be on a leash here.

To return, backtrack about 0.8 mile to the intersection with the Grave-yard Ridge Trail. Turn right here to make a loop, walking through a field where people often camp, and come to a stream crossing that will require some hefty rock hopping after a heavy rain. The trail leads through a narrow, lush forest of ferns and rhododendron back to the southern end of the parking area for a loop of about 3.5 miles. Alternatively, backtrack to the footbridge crossing of the Yellowstone for a steep climb to your original starting point.

12. Devils Courthouse and Little Sam Trail

Round-trip: 4.2 miles
Hiking time: 2 hours
Best time to hike: Late spring, summer, and fall
High point: 5760 feet
Elevation gain: 300 feet
Difficulty: Strenuous
Rules and fees: Dogs must be on a leash on National Park Service property
Maps: USGS Sam Knob; Pisgah Ranger District
Contact: Blue Ridge Parkway headquarters, 828-271-4779; automated road and weather conditions, 828-298-0398; *www.nps.gov/blri;* Pisgah Ranger District, Pisgah National Forest, 828-877-3265; *www.cs.unca.edu/nfsnc*

Getting there: Take the Blue Ridge Parkway to milepost 422, about 14 miles south of the Mount Pisgah area, just past the Devils Courthouse Tunnel on the left. If coming from the south, milepost 422 is 1 mile north of the intersection with NC 215.

According to Cherokee legend, Devils Courthouse is the home of the giant Judaculla, who sat in judgment over the morals of mortals. From the parking lot you can look up at this imposing, impressive rock face, with a summit elevation of 5760 feet, and imagine from its stern, rugged features all sorts of mythical tales.

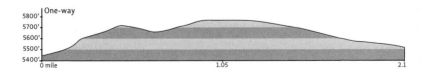

Glenna and Greg walk their yellow Lab, Blaze, up the steep trail to Devils Courthouse.

The short trail to the top of the Devils Courthouse is a very steep, 1-mile round-trip on a mostly paved path. To savor the views and the beauty of the area, the trail can be combined with the Mountains-to-Sea Trail and other Sam Knob area trails to create a scenic hike and a good workout. This is rugged hiking country, so make sure your dog is up to the challenge, and bring extra snacks and water for her.

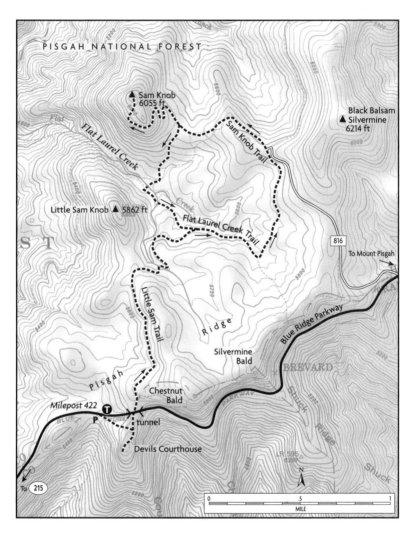

Start the hike by walking back up the parkway toward the tunnel and enter the trail on the right, walking on a paved path. It immediately feels Canada-like, as you walk among tall spruce and hemlock, rhododendron, and other evergreens.

At 0.3 mile, there is an entrance to a spur trail on the left, by a pretty mountain view. This is the trail you will take later, after a stop at the Devils Courthouse summit. The pavement ends here. Continue on the summit trail, and soon start climbing stone stairs to a walled observation area at 5720 feet. Most visitors make this their destination—and you might be content to do so. On a clear, sunny day, the views are priceless. Sight markers help you pick out the distant landmarks, including Great Smoky Mountains National Park 47 miles to the northwest and Sam Knob 2 miles north. You can climb up some boulders for an even better view, but all that dogs will see is a high rock wall. Devils Courthouse contains some of the most sensitive habitats along the parkway. Signs near the trail warn people to stay on trails to help protect endangered plants in the area. Make sure that dogs do the same.

While this summit area is for the humans, head into the forest for the dogs. Backtrack to the spur trail, on the right, and enter the woods following a blue blaze. The trail is soft for paws, but with a high average rainfall it is often very muddy. Be aware that you are now leaving National Park Service property and entering the Pisgah National Forest, where hunting is allowed from September through April. This is a beautiful area that offers lots to sniff and see for dogs, but they should be on a leash and wearing blaze orange during hunting season.

After walking 0.7 mile from the parking area, come to a fork with the Mountains-to-Sea Trail, blazed with a white circle, running to the left and right. Take the right trail and soon cross a stream on a sturdy wooden footbridge. Water-loving dogs will most likely take the wet route across.

At about 1 mile, arrive at a fork with the Little Sam Trail, which veers to the left while the Mountains-to-Sea Trail continues right, heading several miles into the Graveyard Fields area. Turn left here onto the yellow-blazed Little Sam Trail, which follows an old railroad grade north and east for 1.3 miles and connects with the Flat Laurel Creek Trail loop (Hike 21).

Continue on Little Sam over large rocks through deep woods of spruce, birch, mountain ash, and rhododendron tunnels as you walk along Chestnut Bald Ridge. Picturesque mountain views are plentiful, including, at about 1.5 miles, Mount Hardy to the west.

At 1.8 miles, arrive at a fork, bearing left on Little Sam. Moments after the fork, come to a fast-moving creek with no bridge, which calls for a rock hop. The creek is wide but shallow enough that most medium to large dogs should have no problem crossing.

At 2 miles, enter a boulder garden and pass a high rock face on the right. Footing can be precarious and muddy after a rain, and in some places the trail is very rocky and so narrow there is barely room to put two feet together. At 2.4 miles, come to a fork with the Flat Laurel Creek Trail, leading left to the summit of Sam Knob, about 3 miles beyond. This would be a good point to backtrack to Devils Courthouse.

13. Richland Balsam Nature Loop Trail

Loop: 1.4 miles
Hiking time: 1 hour
Best time to hike: Spring through fall, Blue Ridge Parkway road
    conditions permitting
High point: 6410 feet
Elevation gain: 390 feet
Difficulty: Moderate
Rules and fees: Dogs must be on a leash no longer than 6 feet
Map: USGS Sam Knob
Contact: Blue Ridge Parkway headquarters, 828-471-4779; automated
    road and weather conditions, 828-298-0398; *www.nps.gov/blri*

Getting there: From Waynesville, take US 74 west to the Blue Ridge
Parkway entrance. Head north about 12 miles to milepost 431. Turn left
at the Haywood-Jackson Overlook. The trail starts at the southern end
of the parking area on a paved path.

The Richland Balsam Nature Loop Trail is relatively short, but combined
with the Waterrock Knob Trail (Hike 14), another short but steep hike
20 miles farther south on the Blue Ridge Parkway, the two trails make a
complete day of hiking and sightseeing.

Starting at an already lofty elevation of 6020 feet, Richland Balsam
is a great warm-weather hike since it tends to be cool even in summer,
making it suitable for large or long-haired dogs. It is just about 0.5 mile
north of the Richland Balsam Overlook, which is the highest point on
the Blue Ridge Parkway at 6047 feet elevation.

Take a moment before heading out on the trail to absorb the view
from the parking area. The high peaks of the Shining Rock Wilderness

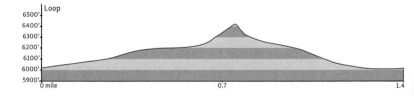

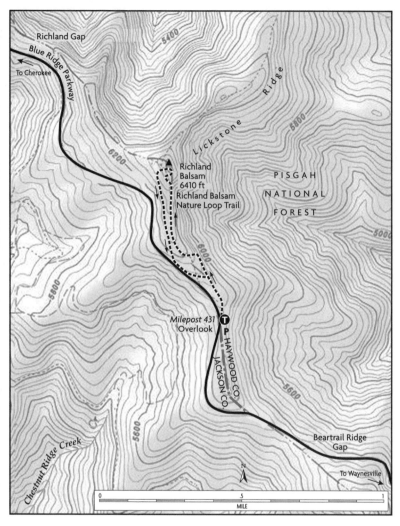

moving in and out of clouds are quite stunning from this vantage point. Start the hike on a paved path at the trailhead sign at the southern end of the overlook, which is named for its position on the Haywood-Jackson county line. The trail was built as a self-guiding nature loop with numbered posts that correspond to descriptions of natural features in a trail brochure. Severe National Park Service budget cuts have forced the parkway office to discontinue printing the brochures, although the posts remain.

At its high elevation of 6410 feet, the Richland Balsam Trail is usually cool in summer.

The trail starts climbing in a spruce–fir forest with many of the same problems afflicting the Fraser firs here as on Mount Mitchell (see Hike 4 for further explanation). At 0.15 mile, come to a fork by a bench and a sign that says, "3100 Feet to the Summit." You can go either way, but take the right loop for a slightly less steep ascent to the summit. Continue climbing, and at 0.3 mile come to another wooden bench. The trail is often wet and overgrown, noticeably left to nature's own devices compared to the other well-used and well-maintained trails off the Blue Ridge Parkway. The buildup of forest floor litter makes soft padding for dogs' paws, and the dense overhead canopy keeps the trail cool and shaded in summer. Fallen moss- and fungus-covered logs are strewn throughout the forest amid maple, birch, spruce, and fir trees. The lush and ancient aspects of this high mountain hike are slightly reminiscent of a walk in the woods of the Pacific Northwest.

At 0.65 mile, begin a steep push uphill over wet, slippery, moss-covered rocks. Emerge at 0.75 mile at the Richland Balsam Mountain summit—with a sign announcing its height at 6410 feet. The little summit area is closed in by large, droopy evergreens so it is hard to glimpse a view, but there is a bench for resting. There are no creeks or springs along the way, so you will need to bring drinking water for the dogs who join you.

Cross the summit area to continue the loop trail back down through the forest. The return trail is quite narrow and rocky, and it can be slippery on the steep descent. At 1.3 miles, come to an overlook with views to the right over the parkway. Just after this lookout is a sign for the parking area. Turn right here and continue to the trailhead.

14. Waterrock Knob Trail

Round-trip: 1.2 miles
Hiking time: 1 hour
Best time to hike: Spring through fall, Blue Ridge Parkway road
   conditions permitting
High point: 6292 feet
Elevation gain: 412 feet
Difficulty: Strenuous
Rules and fees: Dogs must be on a leash no longer than 6 feet
Map: USGS Sylva North
Contact: Blue Ridge Parkway headquarters, 828-471-4779; automated
   road and weather conditions, 828-298-0398; *www.nps.gov/blri*

Getting there: From the Cherokee or Maggie Valley area, take US 19 east to the Blue Ridge Parkway entrance at milepost 455. Head north for 4 miles and turn left at the Waterrock Knob Visitor Center sign. From Waynesville, take US 74 west to the Blue Ridge Parkway entrance. Head south about 8 miles to milepost 451 and turn right at Waterrock Knob. The trail starts at the end of the parking area on a paved path.

Waterrock Knob is a short trail that seems twice as long as it is, thanks to the steep elevation gain, but the scenery is worth the workout. This is one only for hardy dogs who can climb and hop up and across large rocks. If done in the same day as the Richland Balsam Nature Trail Loop,

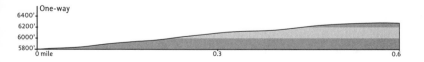

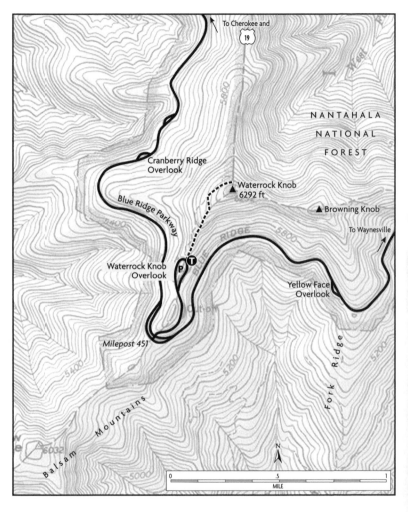

located 20 miles farther north on the Blue Ridge Parkway, it is a great way to see the scenic, high-elevation area of the parkway and get a good leg stretch for you and the dogs.

The trail starts at the Waterrock Knob visitor center, a somewhat rustic outpost that has pit toilets—the only public restrooms at this end of the parkway—and offers books and maps for sale from May through October. It is worth stopping here just for the majestic vistas right from the parking lot. The Blue Ridge Parkway can be seen snaking through the high peaks of the Plott Balsams, a view framed by spruce and fir, reminiscent of New England or Canada. The elevation here—5820 feet—can make for windy, chilly conditions at any time of year, but when the temperature is soaring down in the lower elevations of Cherokee, Waynesville, and Asheville, it is almost always cooler at Waterrock Knob.

Start the hike at the trailhead sign to the right of the visitor center, on a paved path lined with rhododendron, berry bushes, and various evergreens. This is a calf-killer climb that starts steeply from the get-go, but the pavement makes footing easier.

At 0.2 mile, come to a bench and then climb a set of stone stairs. Top out at an overlook with a stone wall that gives way to great views. This is the end of the paved trail. If your dog's legs are up for the challenge,

After a short but very steep ascent, the views are the reward at the summit of Waterrock Knob.

continue across the platform to another set of stairs to a dirt trail. The trail becomes narrow and extremely rocky. You will need both hands in some places to hoist yourself up and over boulders. Agile dogs with good footing should not have a problem, but bring drinking water and snacks for them; there is no reliable water source along the trail.

Reach a bench at 0.6 mile and the Waterrock Knob summit at 6292 feet. You can continue a few more yards through the woods to a large rock outcropping, but it has a dangerous drop-off. Instead, the bench is a nice stopping point to enjoy a drink and a dog treat, and on a clear day there are some good views through the trees. Backtrack from here, going slowly on the descent to the parking area.

Dogs will probably sniff out sights along the trail, such as this toad, before you do.

OTHER WESTERN NORTH CAROLINA MOUNTAINS HIKES

15. Joyce Kilmer Memorial Trail

Loop: 2 miles
Hiking time: 1 hour
Best time to hike: Year-round, weather conditions permitting
High point: 2600 feet
Elevation gain: 320 feet
Difficulty: Moderate
Rules and fees: Dogs are not required to be on a leash, except between
   April 1 and August 15; however, because of high visitation, rangers
   strongly advise hikers to keep dogs on a leash year-round
Maps: USGS Santeetlah Creek and Joyce Kilmer–Slickrock Wilder-
   ness and Citico Creek Wilderness
Contact: Cheoah Ranger District, Nantahala National Forest,
   828-479-6431; *www.cs.unca.edu/nfsnc*

Getting there: From Robbinsville in Graham County, turn onto NC 143 west (Massey Branch Road) and drive about 12 miles. Turn right onto Joyce Kilmer Road (NC 1134) and drive 2 miles. Turn left at the sign for the Joyce Kilmer Memorial Forest and to a parking area at the trailhead.

The Joyce Kilmer–Slickrock Wilderness is a long drive from just about anywhere, sitting at the state's western edge almost to the Tennessee border. But this lush little pocket of the Nantahala National Forest offers a hike that is not to be missed.

One of the oldest virgin forests in the eastern United States—this tract of forest was spared from logging in the 1930s thanks to some conservation-minded Forest Service managers—the super-size trees offer an awesome natural tourist attraction. The wilderness designation means no motorized vehicles, no mechanical equipment, and no bicycles are allowed, further adding to the forest's unique tranquility.

Most hikers walk through the lush, figure-eight trail looking upward, much like tourists gawking at skyscrapers in big cities. Here, some of the old-growth eastern hemlocks and tulip poplars are more than 400 years old. They reach more than 100 feet tall and have girths up to 20 feet in diameter, making you want to wrap your arms around these gentle giants.

The softly rolling trail that crosses streams and has hard-packed earth for mostly easy footing is great for dogs. Game lands surround the forest, though, so during the September through March hunting season people and dogs should wear something blaze orange or consider hiking on Sunday, when hunting is prohibited in the state.

The trail is actually composed of two loops—the lower 1.25-mile Joyce Kilmer Memorial Trail and the upper 0.75-mile Poplar Cove Trail. At the edge of the parking area behind the trailhead signboard, start the Joyce Kilmer Memorial Trail, which was named, appropriately, for Alfred Joyce Kilmer, author of the famous poem "Trees." Cross a bridge and ascend steps into a dense forest of rhododendron and pine trees.

At 0.2 mile, cross another little bridge and walk among eastern hemlocks and under the large, fanlike leaves of Fraser magnolias. The trail climbs and narrows and at 0.5 mile arrives at the intersection with the upper loop and the Joyce Kilmer Memorial—a boulder with a plaque dedicated to Alfred Joyce Kilmer, who was killed in action during World War I.

You can go either way here, but to create one large loop, bear left onto the Poplar Cove loop to continue hiking the trail in a clockwise direction. Here you will start to see massive poplars and hemlocks, some still standing proudly, some toppled by storms, wind, and lightning, and lying on their sides. After about 1 mile, the trail curves in a northeasterly

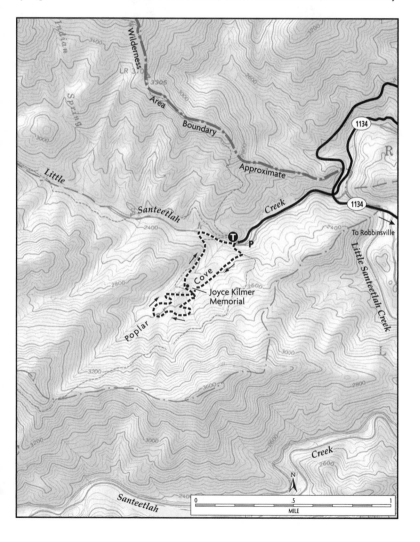

Karen and John feel small beside the giant, old-growth trees in Joyce Kilmer Memorial Forest.

direction and Little Santeetlah Creek will be running to the left. Dog-woods, sourwoods, and maples intermingle with the wise old poplars and hemlocks.

At about 1.25 miles arrive back at the loop intersection and turn left by the memorial rock. In another 0.25 mile, descend wood stairs into a rhododendron tunnel and start to hear the water rushing below. Cross a wood bridge with beautiful views of Little Santeetlah on either side, and in 2 miles arrive back at the trailhead.

16. Rufus Morgan Falls Trail

Loop: 1 mile
Hiking time: 40 minutes
Best time to hike: Year-round, weather and road conditions permitting
High point: 3600 feet
Elevation gain: 470 feet
Difficulty: Moderate
Rules and fees: Dogs must be on a leash between April 1 and August 15, but must be under control at all times
Maps: USGS Wayah Bald; Trails Illustrated Nantahala and Cullasaja Gorges
Contact: Wayah Ranger District, Nantahala National Forest, 828-524-6441; *www.cs.unca.edu/nfsnc*

Getting there: From Franklin, at the intersection with US 441/23, take US 64 west for almost 4 miles to Old Murphy Road. Turn right, and then take the next left onto Wayah Road (NC 1310). Drive 6.3 miles along a narrow, curvy road to Forest Service Road 388, on the left. Take this gravel road for 2 miles to the parking area pullout at the trailhead on the right.

It might have an unusual name, in an out-of-the-way place, deep in the heart of the Nantahala National Forest, but Rufus Morgan Falls is a little gem of a trail that is worth the trek. The pooches will be pleased with the softly padded path and the numerous stream crossings and water sources.

Start the trail just to the right of the trailhead sign, following the blue rectangular blaze, and start climbing immediately up steep switchbacks. The trail starts off on a narrow, often muddy and slick path, framed in beech and buckeye trees as you walk along a ridge with the Left Prong of Rough Fork rushing by on the left.

At 0.2 mile, hop on rocks across the small, shallow stream, turning to the left. In another 0.1 mile, come to an opening in the forest with big

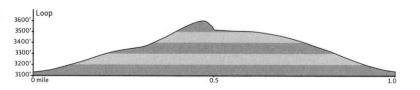

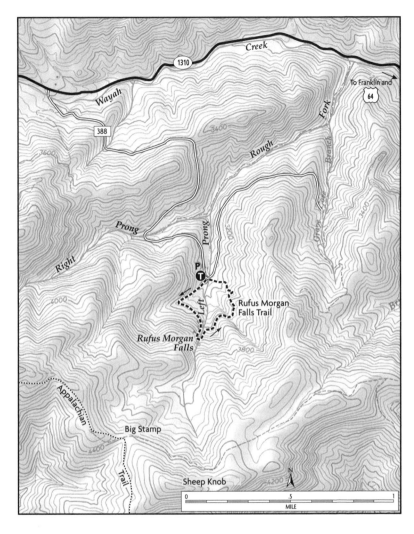

slabs of rocks sliding down to the left. Continue across the rocks and you will start to hear the rush of the falls in the distance.

The trail is a pretty one throughout spring, summer, and fall with an abundance of wildflowers blooming in this moist and shady environment. Lots of fluffy ferns carpet the understory, and large oak trees, as well as maples, birches, and tulip poplars, tower overhead. Just about any time of year you should have the trail to yourself.

At about 0.4 mile come to a wooden bridge over Left Prong, just in front of a small cascade. Dogs will most likely take the water route across, which is shallow enough for large dogs to navigate safely. Cross the bridge and climb up along the side of the stream, walking carefully since it is a steep passage with slick rocks. When the trail levels off, you will be at a fork. Take the sharp right to continue to the base of Rufus Morgan Falls. Dogs can go for a splash and take a drink beneath the lofty falls in a small shallow pool that is hedged in by large rocks, so they cannot roam, or float, too far. The waterfall itself is more of a scenic destination for people to enjoy as it sprays some 70 feet down a sheer rock face.

After spending time in this tranquil spot, backtrack to the intersection and take the right fork to form a loop trail. At 0.7 mile, come to the creek yet again, and cross it with a small rock hop. Enter a dense forest of rhododendron and mountain laurel, walking along an often wet trail with slippery rocks as you descend in elevation.

Soon come out onto a grassy, open field. This eastern part of the loop was thinned through a timber sale, and the loop trail was built with

A small bridge crosses the Left Prong of Rough Fork on the way to Rufus Morgan Falls.

funds from timber sale proceeds. After hiking 1 mile from the start, the trail ends at a Forest Service gate, just south of the parking area. Turn to the left to return to your vehicle. In case you were wondering, the trail is named for the Reverend Albert Rufus Morgan of Asheville, who died in 1983 and was known for his love of the mountains and their hiking trails.

17. Bartram Trail—Jones Gap to Whiterock Mountain

Round-trip: 4.6 miles

Hiking time: 2.5 hours

Best time to hike: Spring through fall, weather and road conditions permitting

High point: 4622 feet

Elevation gain: 462 feet

Difficulty: Moderate

Rules and fees: Dogs must be on a leash between April 1 and August 15, but must be under control at all times

Maps: USGS Scaly Mountain; Bartram Trail, Section 2 (Hickory Gap to Buckeye Creek)

Contact: Highlands Ranger District, Nantahala National Forest, 828-526-3765; *www.cs.unca.edu/nfsnc*; North Carolina Bartram Trail Society, *info@ncbartramtrail.org, www.ncbartramtrail.org*

Getting there: Traveling from Highlands, at the corner of 4th and Main streets, take US 64/28 north and west toward Franklin for 4.2 miles to Turtle Pond Road (SR 1620). Turn left and drive 1.1 miles to Dendy Orchard Road (SR 1678). Turn right and drive 1.4 miles to the top of a hill. This road soon turns to dirt and gravel. Turn left onto Jones Gap Road (Forest Service Road 4522), another dirt road, which can be rutted and muddy after a rain. Drive another 2 miles to the parking area.

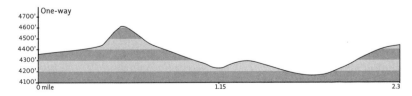

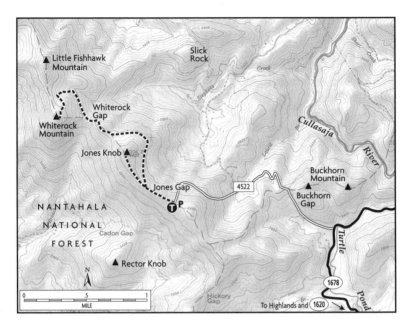

The Bartram Trail is one of North Carolina's long-distance trails and one of the state's great hiking treasures. The trail stretches 100 miles starting in South Carolina, passing into Georgia, and ending in the Nantahala National Forest of North Carolina. The many access points can help you slice up the trail into perfect day-hike portions. Built in honor of Philadelphia naturalist William Bartram, who traveled through the region from 1773 to 1777 chronicling local plants and wildlife, the trail was conceived and is maintained by the North Carolina Bartram Trail Society.

A moderate hike with a couple of spur trails that lead to summit views is the section of the Bartram that starts at Jones Gap and travels northwest to Whiterock Mountain for an out-and-back hike. Start to the right of the trailhead sign, in the direction of Buckeye Gap, 8.5 miles away. Pass a Forest Service gate and follow yellow rectangular blazes down a trail lined in wildflowers and large oak and hickory trees.

At 0.2 mile, enter a field dotted with red clover and soon come to a trail fork and sign pointing left to Jones Knob in 0.3 mile and right to the Bartram Trail. Take the Jones Knob spur trail to the left, following a blue rectangular blaze.

Begin a rapid ascent on a narrow, rocky, and often muddy path heavily lined with such lush undergrowth as ferns, goldenrod, and snakeroot and an abundance of mushrooms that dogs will no doubt sniff out.

Top out on Jones Knob at an altitude of 4622 feet, where large slabs of moss-covered rocks are ringed in oak, rhododendron, and mountain laurel. Head to the left and down through the trees for an opening onto views of the Nantahala Mountains to the west. Backtrack 0.3 mile to the intersection and turn left, back onto the Bartram Trail.

The trail conveys a definite wilderness feel as it passes through dense rhododendron tunnels and gets wrapped up in majestic oaks, pines, and maples as it hugs mountain ledges. Hidden from the high tourist-traffic corridor of nearby US 64's popular waterfalls, Bartram Trail is a perfect place for peace and solitude, even in fall.

Even if the hiking party is just you and the dogs, make some chatter to alert wildlife since bears do roam this area. Hunting is allowed in season, so be prepared with blaze orange vests or clothing for both people and dogs.

At 1.5 miles, start to descend on a steep grade with often-slippery rocks and mud. At about 1.95 miles, arrive at Whiterock Gap—at 4160 feet, the lowest elevation on this section of trail, it is a flat area suitable for

Even when cloudy, the views are pretty from Jones Knob, a stop along the Bartram Trail in the Nantahala National Forest.

camping with a nearby water source at Stevens Creek. Continue on the Bartram Trail, now winding and starting to climb out of the gap.

At 2.25 miles, come to another sign for a water source, and soon after arrive at a fork for a side trail to Whiterock Mountain, following a blue blaze to the left. Take this trail, starting to climb, passing over a sloping rock slab, and in 0.3 mile coming upon more rock masses. Follow the blue-painted blazes to arrive at an awesome overlook. You will definitely want to take this hike on a clear day to get the full effect of this portal onto the sweeping splendor of the Nantahala Mountains.

The rock boulders take some time to climb over into a good vantage point and picnicking position, but still, there are no guard rails, so be careful here that dogs do not run ahead. While the Bartram Trail continues on many, many more miles, this is a good place to backtrack to Jones Gap for a day hike.

18. Cedar Rock Trail via Corn Mill Shoals and Big Rock Trails—DuPont State Forest

Round-trip: 2.75 miles
Hiking time: 1.5 hours
Best time to hike: Year-round
High point: 3060 feet
Elevation gain: 420 feet
Difficulty: Moderate
Rules and fees: Dogs must be on a leash and under control at all times
Maps: USGS Brevard; DuPont State Forest
Contact: DuPont State Forest, 828-877-6527; *www.dupontforest.com*

Getting there: From Brevard, take US 64 east for 3.7 miles. At the Texaco station in Penrose turn right onto Crab Creek Road. Go 4.3 miles and turn right onto DuPont Road, which becomes Staton Road, which then becomes Buck Forest Road. Drive about 5 miles, passing the Hooker Falls parking lot on the right, then the Buck Forest parking area on the left. At the stop sign, turn left onto Cascade Lake Road. Drive 0.8 mile and park at the Corn Mill Shoals Access Area on the right.

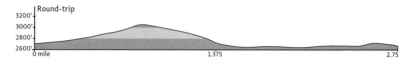

The DuPont State Forest, which was purchased by the state in 1996 and opened to the public in 1997, is still acquiring more land. With trails still being built and a visitor center slated to open in fall 2007, it is a scenic work in progress. Situated on the border of Henderson and Transylvania Counties, the forest is home to some of the prettiest country, riddled with waterfalls, lakes, trout streams, rock outcroppings, and mountain vistas. Unlike a state park, the forest is used for timber management, fishing, and hunting, as well as hiking and mountain biking.

Some of the forest's most popular hiker highlights are the waterfall trails, which are featured in this book (see Hikes 19 and 20), and more than 10,000 acres of land with more than 80 miles of roads and trails to be explored. The views from the Cedar Rock Trail are some of the best to be savored. To get there, hike a loop formed by combining parts of several trails.

Start at the Corn Mill Shoals Access Area and cross Cascade Lake Road. Enter the woods at the sign for Corn Mill Shoals Road, which bears to the right. Walk about 0.1 mile and turn left onto the Big Rock Trail. This is a deeply rutted trail, also used by mountain bikers, and is dotted with large rocks that dogs will need to be able to hop up on.

Keep climbing amid heavy rhododendron and mountain laurel growth, along with white pine and hemlock, sassafras and hickory, and oak, maple, and holly. At 0.5 mile, arrive at an elevation of about 2900 feet and an opening in the woods onto big slabs of granite, surrounded by pitch pines.

This hike is great at any time of year, but for some truly remarkable views try it in fall when flaming red maples and scarlet oaks dot these rock outcrops and the forested mountainsides look like a giant-size crayon box come alive with color.

Continue northeast up the big rock slabs following unusual blazes—rock piles, known as cairns, show the way, instead of colored markings on trees. The granite domes are part of the DuPont Dedicated Nature Preserve, so visitors must stay on the marked trails to prevent damage to the unique plant community found here.

Follow the cairns to again enter a pitch pine and oak forest. At 0.9 mile, emerge from the woods onto another granite overlook, and

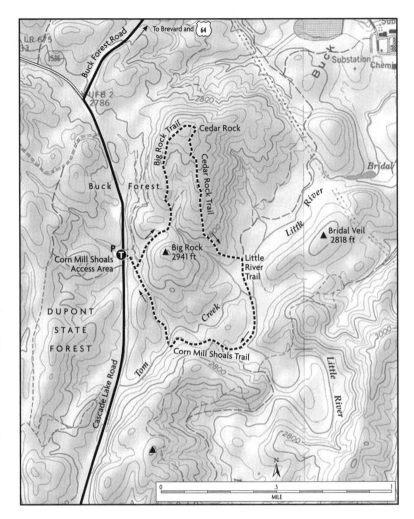

continue to the trailhead sign and T intersection with the Cedar Rock Trail, which runs to the left and right. To make a loop, turn right here and head south across a large expanse of pothole-riddled rock, which after a rain will have collected little pools of water. Keep in mind that this area is exposed to the sun, so it can be very hot in summer on furry heads and little paws.

Continue descending, to the feast of more wide-open mountain scenery, and at 1.4 miles, start carefully down a very steep, slick rock section with poor traction. This lasts for about 0.2 mile and bottoms out at a fork with the Little River Trail. Turn right here.

Rock piles, known as cairns, show the way along the Cedar Rock Trail in DuPont State Forest.

After crossing a wood bridge over a small creek, the trail widens out onto a gravel road, heading south. You will be walking in a cool, shady forest of tall white pines, hemlocks, and maples and on a carpet of pine needles scattered over gravel. At about 2 miles, arrive at an intersection with the Corn Mill Shoals Trail. Turn right. (If you go left here, you will arrive at the shoals in 0.3 mile.)

Pass by the turnoff to the Burnt Mountain Trail on the left and keep walking on a path of alternating hard-packed dirt and gravel road. In about 0.75 mile, come to the fork with the Big Rock Trail. Stay to the left and head back to the parking area on Cascade Lake Road.

19. Hooker Falls Trail— DuPont State Forest

Round-trip: 0.75 mile
Hiking time: 20 minutes
Best time to hike: Year-round
High point: 2275 feet
Elevation gain: 35 feet
Difficulty: Easy
Rules and fees: Dogs must be on a leash and under control at all times
Maps: USGS Standingstone Mountain; DuPont State Forest
Contact: DuPont State Forest office, 828-877-6527; *www.dupontforest.com*

Getting there: From Brevard, take US 64 east for 3.7 miles. At the Texaco station in Penrose turn right onto Crab Creek Road. Go 4.3 miles and turn right onto DuPont Road. Drive 3.1 miles to the Hooker Falls parking lot on the right.

The DuPont State Forest is one of the state's newest recreation areas, created in 1996 from land purchased from the DuPont Company. Work on trail construction and improvement, as well as bridges, overlooks, picnic areas, and other amenities, is ongoing.

The sprawling forest straddles the Transylvania–Henderson county line and lies close to the South Carolina border. The area is pure outdoor heaven—encompassing 10,400 acres of lush forests, scenic vistas, lakes and rivers, and spectacular waterfalls. Wildlife, wildflowers, fish, and birds are also abundant, providing outdoor excitement for people as well as dogs. Hunting by permit is allowed on specific days from September through May. Check the DuPont State Forest website for the designated hunting days.

There are many trails of varying length and difficulty. Two scenic trails—the Triple Falls Trail, which climbs to Triple Falls and High Falls (Hike 20) and a loop around the Cedar Rock Trail (Hike 18)—are also described in this book. For those people and pups who are looking for natural beauty and a day outdoors but not so much strenuous climbing, Hooker Falls Trail is the perfect choice. The distance is short enough and the terrain level enough to accommodate strollers and wheelchairs,

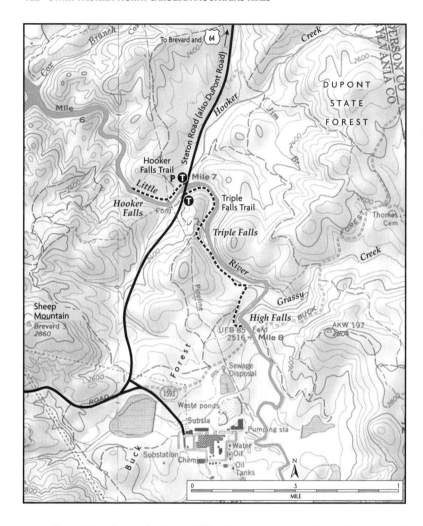

as well as older dogs who have difficulty on steep, rocky trails, or small breeds whose little legs cannot hike very far.

Start at the southern end of the Hooker Falls parking lot by a gated road. Go around the gate and start walking along the wide gravel-and-dirt Hooker Falls Road. Bear left at the first fork you come to and continue walking along the Little River. In spring, dogs love sniffing the many wildflowers along the trail edges. The tall hardwood trees, as well as evergreens and rhododendron thickets, provide a shady path. This is also a suitable summer hike since the trail is short and fairly level and dogs can get up close to the river in numerous places. Picnic tables are scattered in the woods, close to the trail.

Fall, as it is throughout much of the state, is also a beautiful hiking season. But the word is out, and since the DuPont State Forest is so popular in fall, weekends from late September through early November can be crowded on the trail. Try a weekday, or hike here in the off-season, for more tranquility.

In a few minutes you will approach the top of Hooker Falls, where you can admire the waterfall from a small overlook. Continue straight on the path and arrive, at 0.35 mile, at the pool below. Hooker Falls, the site of a former grist mill, is a gently flowing cascade, which only drops 13 feet off a natural rock ledge into a large, wide pool below, before running down into Cascade Lake. The pool has an easy access area that beckons people and dogs to dip their toes or wade right in for a quick cooldown. Dogs must remain on a leash here, even when in the water. You can sit on any of the plentiful rocks and tree trunks to take in the sight before retracing your steps to the parking area.

Talley takes a break from swimming in the pool below Hooker Falls in DuPont State Forest.

20. Triple Falls and High Falls Trails—DuPont State Forest

Round-trip: 2.6 miles
Hiking time: 1.5 hours
Best time to hike: Spring and fall
High point: 2600 feet
Elevation gain: 400 feet
Difficulty: Moderate
Rules and fees: Dogs must be on a leash and under control of the owner
Maps: USGS Standingstone Mountain; DuPont State Forest
Contact: DuPont State Forest office, 828-877-6527; *www.dupontforest.com*

Getting there: From Brevard, take US 64 east for 3.7 miles. At the Texaco station in Penrose turn right onto Crab Creek Road. Go 4.3 miles and turn right onto DuPont Road. Drive 3.1 miles to the Hooker Falls parking lot on the right. Park here and cross Staton Road, head south, walk across the bridge, and then descend the stairs on the left to the trailhead for Triple Falls.

There are so many miles of trails in the sprawling natural area of the Du-Pont State Forest, it is hard to choose, so three trails are described in this book (Hikes 18, 19, and 20). Possibly the most popular—for both dogs and people, is this one: the Triple Falls Trail. Quick and to the point—it brings you through some of the prettiest parts of the forest on a steep but fast trail to see some of the loveliest waterfalls.

The best times of year to hike this trail are in spring when wildflowers are profuse and in fall when the colorful leaves framing the waterfalls make for postcard-perfect scenery. Be aware that the forest allows hunting by permit only. Seasons are established for deer, turkey, and small game hunting from September through May. Although hunting safety zones are established in areas of high visitor traffic, such as the waterfalls

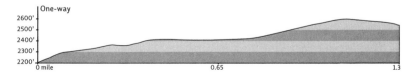

Arlene and Shelby take a look at High Falls, one of many waterfalls in DuPont State Forest.

trails, you should put a blaze orange handkerchief or vest on your dog during hunting season.

Starting at the trailhead, descend some stairs and walk through a wooden "turnstile" for keeping out bikes and horses, then ascend a wide gravel path thickly lined with rosebay rhododendron and mountain laurel. The Little River flows to the left, where you are likely to see fishermen in waders during spring, summer, and fall.

The trail starts to rise rapidly after about 0.1 mile. Although the hike is less than 3 miles long, you will work up a thirst. Bring extra water for dogs to have whenever they need it. Especially in summer, this humid area can make you feel even hotter on the inclines. This is a popular trail, so you are likely to encounter many people, dogs, and even school and camp groups. To lessen the chances of encountering trail traffic, hike weekdays, early mornings, or late afternoons. Spring is a great time to hike here since the wildflower population is prolific, including such beauties as bloodroot, violet, trillium, and pink lady's slipper, in addition to the blooms of rhododendron and mountain laurel.

The real payoff on this hike are the waterfalls. The trail leads first to Triple Falls, so named for its three layers of cascading falls. It also is a bit of a movie star—Triple Falls made an appearance in the 1992 Hollywood movie *Last of the Mohicans,* starring Daniel Day-Lewis.

The first view of the 120-foot falls arrives on the left at about 0.2 mile. The vantage point from the trail is great for picture taking, but a short cutoff between the second and third tiers leads down to the river, where you and the dogs can walk out on the large, flat rocks for a closer look at the cascades. This is an extremely steep, gravel trail. A short side trip to the right leads up steps to a picnic shelter.

If you stay on the main trail, you will come to an intersection. The trail to the right leads to Buck Forest Road. Turn left onto the High Falls Trail and continue to an area for viewing this 120-foot, broad-shouldered waterfall at about 1 mile. Walk parallel to the river for about 0.2 mile, then turn right at the next fork. There is a short side trail that leads to the base of the falls, which is a muddy, very steep descent on stairs. Proceed slowly and carefully, especially when arriving at the pool of water at the base. Water running over the rocks makes footing extremely slippery and precarious. This is a good place for dogs to take a drink, cool off their paws, and maybe take a quick dunk, but they must remain on a leash and should not be allowed to swim freely, since it is easy for them to slip quickly downstream.

The hemlock- and pine-framed river, the powerful waterfall rushing overhead, and the view of a covered bridge at the top of the falls all make this a place where you will probably want to linger. Head back up the steep trail, and from here backtrack to the trailhead on Staton Road.

21. Sam Knob Summit and Flat Laurel Creek Trails

Loop: 3.6 miles
Hiking time: 2.5 hours
Best time to hike: Spring, summer, and fall
High point: 6040 feet
Elevation gain: 620 feet
Difficulty: Moderate
Rules and fees: Dogs must be on a leash between April 1 and August 15, but must be under voice control at all times
Map: USGS Sam Knob and National Geographic Trails Illustrated Map, Pisgah Ranger District

Contact: Pisgah Ranger District, Pisgah National Forest, 828-877-3265; *www.cs.unca.edu/nfsnc;* Blue Ridge Parkway headquarters, 828-271-4779; automated road and weather conditions, 828-298-0398; *www.nps.gov/blri*

Getting there: At the intersection with US 64 and US 276 in Brevard, take US 276 north into the Pisgah National Forest. Drive about 14 miles, staying on US 276, to the Blue Ridge Parkway. Head south on the parkway for about 8 miles to just past milepost 420. Turn right onto Forest Service Road 816. Drive 1.2 miles to the parking area where you will see signboards and restrooms. The trailhead for Sam Knob is to the right of the restrooms.

The Sam Knob Summit Trail is an out-and-back trail to a perfect picture-taking spot on a high-elevation knob. Or, you can create a loop trail by combining the Sam Knob with the Flat Laurel Creek Trail, which is the trail described here.

Start out on the Sam Knob Trail to the right of the restrooms and almost immediately come to a fork. Stay to the right, following blue blazes that are more often painted on rocks than on tree trunks. Pass along a trail lined with high grasses and such shrubby vegetation as mountain laurel, azalea, rhododendron, and berry bushes, as well as many colorful wildflowers in spring, such as the delicate-looking thyme-leaved bluets, and asters and goldenrod in fall.

At about 0.2 mile, the trail opens onto a sweeping meadow, surrounded by 360 degrees of mountains. This is a lovely, unique, and scenic spot—a high-altitude valley nestled between the rugged mountains of the Middle Prong Wilderness to the west and the Shining Rock Wilderness to the east. Dogs seem to take this opportunity to scout out the trail on their own. If you are hiking during hunting season, generally September through April, keep dogs close by and make sure they are wearing a blaze orange doggy vest.

The initial destination—Sam Knob—juts out of the scenery directly ahead. Walk another 0.5 mile through the meadow and come to a trail sign for the Flat Laurel Creek Trail, which veers left. The Sam Knob Trail

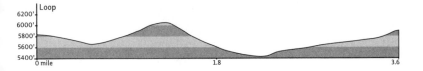

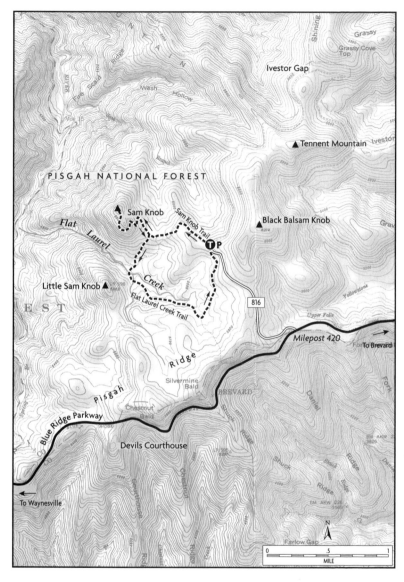

continues to the right. Head right and soon enter a tightly woven rhododendron forest and start climbing switchbacks on a narrow trail.

At about 1.25 miles from the trailhead you will come to a large chunk of white quartz. It offers a good spot for dogs to climb on and for you to take pictures, but just past here is an even better place—the Sam Knob summit at 6040 feet elevation. Here large, flat slabs of exposed rock are great for sitting on and having lunch, resting, and taking in the 360-degree views. But hold on to dogs if they have a tendency to run and lunge—there are steep drop-offs.

Even in summer, at this elevation (the Sam Knob summit is actually 10 feet higher than legendary and nearby Cold Mountain) it can be windy and chilly. Bring extra layers for this hike, as well as drinking water. The climb and thinner air will make dogs and people thirsty.

Mai and Shelby head toward the summit of Sam Knob in the Pisgah National Forest.

After a sufficient time enjoying the views of the West Fork of the Pigeon River valley to the west and the peaks of the Shining Rock Wilderness to the east, including 6214-foot Black Balsam Knob, backtrack on the Sam Knob Trail to its intersection with the Flat Laurel Creek Trail. To create a loop, turn right onto the Flat Laurel Creek Trail.

In a few minutes you will come to the first creek crossing—there is no bridge, but it is easy to rock hop across this great place for dogs to take a drink and cool their paws. The trail continues through alternating woods and rolling grassy meadows. It also continues to cross Flat Laurel Creek, often requiring rock hopping. Camping is allowed on national forest land, so in summer and early fall you will pass by many picturesque campsites dotted with tents.

The trail starts to get rockier—pay attention to dogs with sensitive pads. At about 2.7 miles into the hike you come to an intersection with the Little Sam Trail (see Hike 12), with the yellow-blazed trail branching off to the right. Continue straight on the Flat Laurel Creek Trail. It continues to be rocky as it follows an old logging road through woods of evergreen trees and open fields. At about 3.6 miles, the trail emerges at the parking area.

22. Cold Mountain via Art Loeb Trail

Round-trip: 10.6 miles

Hiking time: 7 hours

Best time to hike: Late spring, summer, and early fall

High point: 6030 feet

Elevation gain: 2800 feet

Difficulty: Strenuous

Rules and fees: Dogs must be leashed between April 1 and August 15, and under voice control; leashing dogs is strongly recommended in wilderness areas year-round

Maps: USGS Cruso; USGS Waynesville; Trails Illustrated Pisgah Ranger District

Contact: Carolina Mountain Club, *www.carolinamtnclub.org;* Pisgah Ranger District, Pisgah National Forest, 828-877-3265; *www .cs.unca.edu/nfsnc*

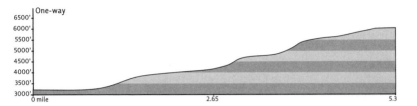

Getting there: Take Interstate 40 west to exit 37/US 23. Continue on US 23 west to Canton. Take the Canton bypass to NC 110 south (which becomes NC 215 east). Turn left onto Little East Fork Road (SR 1129). Camp Daniel Boone will be on the left. Turn here and drive past the camp. Look for the kiosk at the trailhead, where a sign says "Art Loeb Trail," and park on the right.

Cold Mountain—the legendary namesake of the fictional novel and Hollywood movie—is a real place. It is one of the highest peaks in the eastern United States and juts majestically out of the Shining Rock Wilderness Area of the Pisgah National Forest.

Since *Cold Mountain,* the National Book Award–winning novel by Charles Frazier, was published in 1997, and *Cold Mountain,* the movie, was released in 2003, the mountain has been attracting curious adventure seekers, even though the movie was not filmed in North Carolina.

Cold Mountain is not your typical tourist attraction. The 6030-foot summit is accessible only by foot by way of several trails, the "easiest" of which is the nearly 11-mile round-trip hike described here. Forest rangers say that even though interest in the hike has increased, many who attempt the feat are not properly prepared and turn back halfway, discouraged by its difficulty.

If you and your dog are experienced and in-shape hikers, this is a trail worth seeing to the end. Keep in mind, though, that this is for the super trail dog—those pooches who are out of shape, elderly, or have breathing difficulties should not attempt this hike.

Start the hike on the Art Loeb Trail out of Camp Daniel Boone, where the elevation is just over 3200 feet. The climbing starts almost immediately through a thick forest of rosebay rhododendron, mountain laurel, and Carolina hemlock. The steep ascent only lasts about ten minutes, but a lot more climbing is to come—the trail gains nearly 3000 feet of elevation in just over 5 miles.

One of the best times to take this hike is in spring, from mid-March to late April. During this time, the hardwood trees have not yet sprouted their leaves, and so for much of the hike the ultimate destination—the summit of Cold Mountain—is visible through the bare trees. During summer, the heavy leaf cover will obliterate views for the entire hike.

However, spring can also bring the dubious thrill of unpredictable weather, even early spring snowstorms. For all sorts of precipitation possibilities, dress with warm, moisture-wicking layers, a wind- and water-resistant outer jacket for yourself, and bring raingear for your dog. Also be sure to pack a first-aid kit for people and dogs and to bring extra water and food.

This hike requires good map and compass skills—the trail, at least at the start, is well used, but it is not regularly maintained and is not blazed. Cell phone reception is not reliable. Before embarking on this hike, be sure to tell friends where you are going and when you expect to return.

Since the Shining Rock area is a federally designated wilderness, camping is permitted but campfires are not, and groups are limited to ten people. Dogs should be under control at all times.

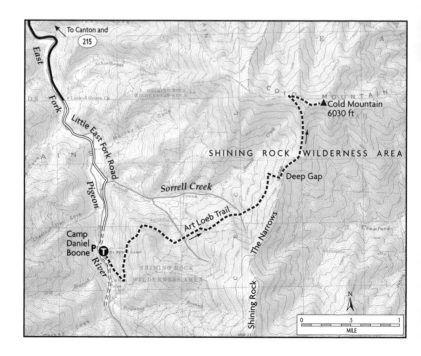

The trail to Cold Mountain, seen in the distance, can often be chilly and snow-covered.

Continue on an often rocky path that hugs the mountainsides with steep ledges and occasional stream crossings. Since no motorized equipment is allowed in the wilderness area, chainsaws are prohibited, making for slow removal of the many large trees that may have fallen across the trail. Hikers will often have to climb over these trees. At about 2 miles the trail crosses Sorrell Creek—a good spot for dogs to take a water break.

At 3.8 miles from the trailhead you will come to a large, level, grassy clearing known as Deep Gap, at 5000 feet elevation. This is a nice resting spot for people and dogs. Be sure to have your dog drink and eat a snack; he will have spent a lot of energy and will need some sustenance for the last push to the summit.

From Deep Gap, take the trail to the left, following a steep northeasterly route to the top. After about 0.5 mile from Deep Gap, a spring of fresh water runs out of the rocks on the trail's right side. This is a good source of drinking water for dogs and for people, as long as it is purified first. At just over 5 miles from the start, a large rock outcropping is on the right—a great place to stop and revel in the views.

You will soon arrive at the summit, marked by a tiny U.S. Geological Survey marker on a rock. The trail comes to a dead end here, with spacious views of the Balsam Mountains, a long ridge running south called The Narrows, and to the southeast the Pisgah National Forest's other tall peaks, including Mount Pisgah, visible for the TV tower jutting from its top.

There is no wide—or safe—place to sit and relax right at the summit. Backtrack to the larger rock outcropping and proceed with extreme caution. Dogs should be on a leash here—there are long drop-offs and no railings, but this is a place where you will definitely be glad your best hiking buddy is with you. The views, not to mention the feeling of accomplishment at climbing this peak with your dog, rival the fictional saga of *Cold Mountain*.

23. Coontree Loop Trail

Loop: 3.7 miles
Hiking time: 2 hours
Best time to hike: Spring through fall
High point: 3300 feet
Elevation gain: 1160 feet
Difficulty: Moderate
Rules and fees: Dogs must be leashed between April 1 and August 15, but must be under voice control at all times
Map: USGS Shining Rock; National Geographic Trails Illustrated Map, Pisgah Ranger District
Contact: Pisgah Ranger District, Pisgah National Forest, 828-877-3265; *www.cs.unca.edu/nfsnc*

Getting there: From Brevard, turn north on US 276 into the Pisgah National Forest. After you come to the ranger station on the right, it is 3 miles to the Coontree Picnic Area on the left. Park here and walk across

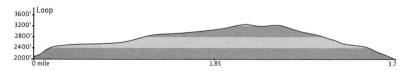

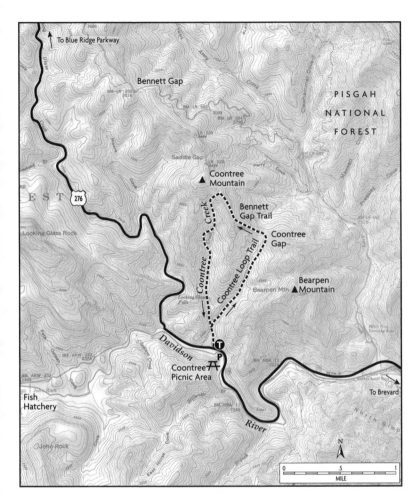

the road to the trailhead. Although this is a national forest, US 276 can be a congested road, especially on weekends. Use caution and make sure your dog is on a leash when crossing this highway.

This is a lovely loop trail for people and their dogs throughout the year. However, it is a trail shared with mountain bikers from October 15 through April 15, so skip hiking it during that time if you want to avoid bikes on the sometimes steep and narrow trails. If hiking during fall (an exceptionally pretty time when the hardwoods turn a variety of brilliant shades), dogs should wear blaze orange vests to distinguish themselves from game animals since hunting is allowed in the forest.

Early spring is actually a great time here because it has warmed up enough for you to enjoy being out on the trail, but it is still cool enough for comfortable hiking. Since the leaves then have not yet filled in this mostly hardwood forest, great ridge-top views are visible through the trees.

Start the Coontree Loop on a level path alongside a small stream. After 0.2 mile the trail splits—both trails are blazed blue, and either of them will bring you around the loop. For easier footing on the hills, take the trail to the right, which runs along a small stream. Follow the blue blazes through a forest of rhododendron, mountain laurel, oak, tulip poplar, hemlock, and pine for about a half mile. The gurgling stream makes for lovely company and offers a great way for dogs to cool off. The pines and hemlocks appear fluffy and rise high and wide, making the trail feel like a snug, sunken little world.

Just after a quick stream crossing—there are several of these on the loop, with either logs or rock hops to get across—is a long, steep climb. At 1.2 miles arrive at Coontree Gap, where the trail forks both left and right at a trailhead sign for Bennett Gap. Turn left and follow the trails, which overlap and are blazed both red and blue, for nearly 1 mile. As you start out on the Bennett Gap Trail in winter and early spring, along the ridge top are wide views off the east and west sides of the trail.

Come to a sign for Coontree Trail and take that to the left, where you will start to descend on steep switchbacks, again following the blue blazes. The trail is narrow and can be muddy and slippery in parts, winding through thick rhododendron and mountain laurel tunnels. Make several more precarious crossings of Coontree Creek on logs (some are very narrow and wobbly). Make sure your dog is not afraid of this type of footing before starting out.

Follow the stream, which will be on the left, down to rejoin the loop. The Coontree Picnic Area, where you parked, sits on the Davidson River and is a nice lunch spot. Several other riverside picnic areas are located both north and south from here on US 276. This area is also full of other great hiking trails for dogs since it is national forest land and dogs are not required to be on a leash. The exception is in the Davidson River Campground and between April 1 and August 15. In all areas you are required to clean up after your pet.

Opposite: *The Coontree Loop Trail offers shaded walking along a stream in the Pisgah National Forest.*

24. Pink Beds Trail

Loop: 3.4 miles
Hiking time: 1.5 hours
Best time to hike: Year-round
High point: 3280 feet
Elevation gain: 100 feet
Difficulty: Easy
Rules and fees: Dogs must be on a leash between April 1 and August 15, but must be under voice control at all times
Map: USGS Shining Rock; National Geographic Trails Illustrated, Pisgah Ranger District
Contact: Pisgah Ranger District, Pisgah National Forest, 828-877-3265; *www.cs.unca.edu/nfsnc*

Getting there: From Brevard, at the intersection of US 64 and US 276, head north onto US 276 into the Pisgah National Forest. Drive about 11 miles, staying on US 276. The Pink Beds Picnic Area and parking will be on the right, just after the Cradle of Forestry in America. The parking area can also be accessed by heading 3.5 miles south on US 276 from the Blue Ridge Parkway at milepost 412.

Start the hike at the northeastern end of the picnic area at the Forest Service trailhead sign behind a gated road. Cross a footbridge over Pigeon Branch and then follow an old gravel road through a wide open field framed in pines, dogwoods, and hemlocks. At about 500 feet, the trail forks. Take the left branch to walk the loop trail in a clockwise direction, following the orange blazes.

The Pink Beds Loop is one of many, many hiking trails in the Pisgah National Forest that welcome dogs. The easily accessible trailhead of the Pink Beds and its relatively little elevation change and many bridge-covered water crossings make it a great playground for dogs of all sizes and activity levels during all seasons of the year.

This is also a trail well populated throughout the year with hikers, dog walkers, and runners. Although leashes are not required, be sure to carry one for times when hiking traffic is high to prevent encounters with other dogs or with people.

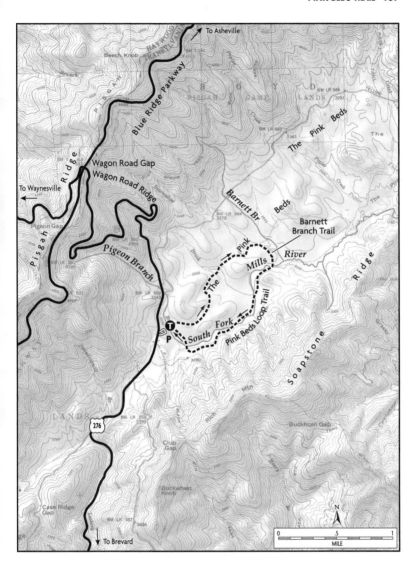

The trail winds intermittently through open meadows of wildflowers and around bogs filled with trout lilies and then narrows into dense
woods of towering hemlocks. Over the years the loop trail has been
shortened—thanks to some busy beavers—from a once 5-mile to a 3-mile
loop. Beavers have built a dam across the creek at the northern end of
the loop, forming a pond and flooding the former trail.

At about 1.3 miles, come to a fork. If you continue straight, you will come to a trail closure sign in about 1 mile. To make a loop, turn right here onto the Barnett Branch Trail, which is blazed in blue (and also is the Mountains-to-Sea Alternate) and follow it for just under 0.5 mile

The many water crossings along the Pink Beds Trail make this a fun hike for dogs.

through deep woods along a creek. At the next intersection, turn right to connect back to the Pink Beds Loop.

This trail continues to crisscross the South Fork of the Mills River several times on sturdy wooden footbridges as it lopes through more meadows and woods of white pine, hemlock, oak, maple, and birch and dense tunnels of rhododendron and mountain laurel. The trail is part of the larger Pink Beds area of the Pisgah National Forest nestled in a lower-lying depression between Pisgah Ridge to the west and Soapstone Ridge to the east. The name likely comes from the proliferation of the bright pink rosebay rhododendron that bloom in June.

Still hugging the South Fork as it gently winds through forest, the trail offers no shortage of water that dogs would love to splash in and drink from. However, the bogs are sensitive areas and are home to many organisms and delicate plants, including wildflowers. Hikers should stay on the designated trail and not enter the water and should make sure dogs do not damage the natural environment.

From the trail junction, continue to follow the orange blazes for another 1.6 miles to arrive back at the trailhead. During rainy seasons, the flat area can collect pools of water in areas. Be sure to wear shoes you don't mind getting wet and bring towels to clean off muddy paws before the ride home. You will also want to bring a picnic to enjoy after the hike since the trailhead is adjacent to the large, well-kept Pink Beds Picnic Area.

25. Cat Gap Loop

Loop: 5 miles
Hiking time: 3 hours
Best time to hike: Year-round
High point: 3380 feet
Elevation gain: 1050 feet
Difficulty: Moderate
Rules and fees: Dogs must be on a leash between April 1 and August 15, but must be under control at all times
Maps: USGS Shining Rock; Trails Illustrated Pisgah National Forest
Contact: Pisgah Ranger District, Pisgah National Forest, 828-479-6431; *www.cs.unca.edu/nfsnc;* Pisgah Center for Wildlife Education, 828-877-4423

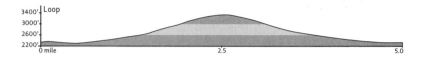

Getting there: From Brevard, turn north onto US 276 into the Pisgah National Forest. Drive about 5 miles, passing the Pisgah District Ranger Station/Visitor Center (which is on the right, is staffed weekdays, and offers area information and maps). Turn left onto Forest Service Road 475 at the sign for the Pisgah Fish Hatchery. Drive 1.5 miles to the fish hatchery and the Pisgah Center for Wildlife Education. Park here. The trail starts at the end of the parking lot opposite the wildlife center.

With a name like "Cat Gap," this is a trail you just have to hike with your dog. Though cats are actually not likely to cross this path, the Cat Gap Loop is riddled with water in the form of rivers, streams, cascades, and puddles, and in spring and summer the many fragrant and colorful wildflowers that come to life along the trail are things that dogs will appreciate maybe just as much as chasing cats.

The slightly easier way to hike the loop is in a clockwise direction to avoid a very steep climb at the outset—although there will be climbing either way you go. While the cooler air of fall and winter is more comfortable for hiking with dogs, the trail passes through game lands, so hunting is permitted. Put a blaze orange vest on your dog during hunting season.

Start the trail at the signboard at the far end of the parking lot. Following orange blazes, enter the woods, and start hiking south along the Davidson River. Cross the first of many footbridges at about 0.1 mile, and follow the trail along the river through a forest of rhododendron, hemlock, oak, and other hardwoods, with campsites scattered through the trees.

At 0.5 mile cross a narrow, split-log bridge and one of many creek crossings that offer a welcome break for dogs to wade in and cool off. Since this is a hike with lots of climbing, bring extra drinking water for your dogs in warm and cool weather—they should not drink surface water too heartily because of the risk of parasites.

The trail starts to widen, and the river fades from sight but can still be heard. At 1 mile arrive at a crossing of lovely Horse Cove Creek but no

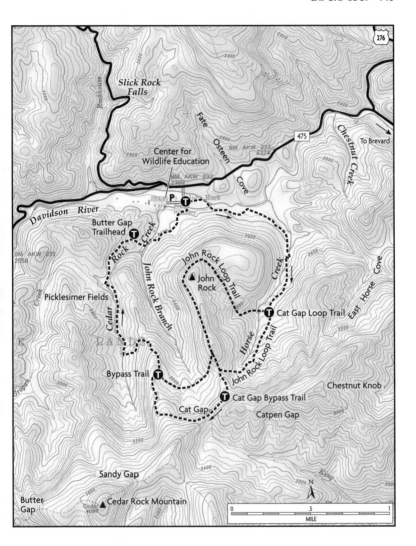

bridge. The water is usually shallow enough to rock hop while keeping your feet dry. Once you're across, the trail starts climbing steadily. After about 0.3 mile, the yellow-blazed John Rock Loop turns to the right. This is a 1.8-mile loop to a high rock outcropping with open views, but the sheer drop-offs make it a little scary for hiking with dogs who bolt and run without warning. To stay on the Cat Gap Loop, keep walking straight. Along the way several trails intersect, so be sure to stick to the orange blazes.

A bridge along Cat Gap Loop

Continue a steady uphill hike, occasionally climbing steps on particularly steep sections. At 2 miles, arrive at the terminus of the John Rock Loop on the right. Turn left and begin another steep stretch before topping out at Cat Gap among a sea of mountain laurel. Even in winter on this ridge top, it is hard to see any views from this point. Keep winding through rhododendron and mountain laurel tunnels, passing large patches of galax on the ground and eventually some mountain views off to the right.

At 2.4 miles, the trail forks—veer to the right and eventually start descending. Come to a fork with the Cat Gap Bypass Trail on the right at about 3 miles, but bear left to continue the loop. At 3.2 miles the trail makes an abrupt left turn and then soon arrives at a wide, shallow stream crossing with no bridge. After crossing, bear to the right and come to a flat area of tall pines and hemlocks with lots of open space beneath the trees. The Davidson River can be heard running off to the right, and in a moment there it is, rushing under a log bridge. After the bridge, turn right and come to a fork with the blue-blazed Butter Gap Trail, which turns to the left and Picklesimer Fields.

Stay to the right, heading toward the sound of water. Descend along cascades on Cedar Rock Creek to the right, and at 4.8 miles arrive at the fork with FR 475C. Turn left on this road, and you'll see the wildlife center and parking area ahead of you.

26. Pulliam Creek Trail

Round-trip: 6.5 miles
Hiking time: 3 hours
Best time to hike: Spring
High point: 2100 feet
Elevation gain: 900 feet
Difficulty: Moderate to strenuous
Rules and fees: Dogs must always be on a leash
Maps: USGS Cliffield Mountain; Environmental and Conservation Organization Trails of the Green River Game Lands
Contact: Environmental and Conservation Organization, 828-692-0385; *www.eco-wnc.org;* North Carolina Wildlife Resources Commission, 919-707-0050; *www.ncwildlife.org*

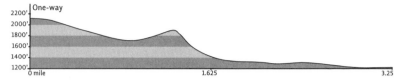

Getting there: From Hendersonville, take Interstate 26 east. Take exit 53/Upward Road. Turn left (east) and go 1.8 miles. Turn right on Big Hungry Road (SR 1802). Go 0.5 mile and turn left, continuing on Big Hungry Road. Go 0.3 mile and turn right, continuing on Big Hungry Road. Go 1.7 miles to the bridge crossing the Big Hungry River. From the bridge, go 2 miles to a small pullout on the right at a Wild Trout Waters sign. The trail descends to the right.

The Green River Game Lands is a beautiful, rugged, natural area of forests, rivers, gorges, and hillsides consisting of more than 10,000 acres along the Green River in Henderson and Polk counties. The area is owned by the state and managed for the primary purpose of wildlife conservation and management, which means that fishing, hunting, and trapping are allowed.

The 16 miles of trails in the Green River Game Lands are jointly maintained by the Environmental and Conservation Organization (a nonprofit group based in Hendersonville) and the North Carolina Wildlife Resources Commission. Hikers should be aware that the hunting season lasts for about eight months, from mid-September through mid-May. Currently, hunting is prohibited in North Carolina on Sunday, so that is a good day to hike. For optimal safety, people and their dogs should wear blaze orange vests or other brightly colored clothing when hiking during hunting season.

All the trails have a sense of the wild—although there are trailhead signs, the trails are not blazed. One of the best trails for dogs is the Pulliam Creek Trail, and one of the best times to hike is in spring, when it is not yet hot and the wildflowers are blooming in abundance.

The Pulliam Creek Trail starts out by crossing a footbridge and then runs side by side with the creek. It first passes through a controlled burn area with many charred trees and stumps on both sides of the trail. Do not be turned off—it only lasts about a half mile.

Once out of the burn area, you are ensconced in wilderness as the trail winds through a moist, shaded river valley and along the dry, sunny sides of steep gorges. The great variation in elevation and environment allows

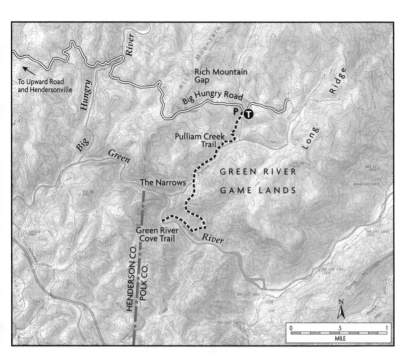

for a wide range of spring wildflowers. In early April, keep an eye on trail edges and hillsides for the white-petaled bloodroot, the bright-red-colored fire pink, a variety of white and purple violets, Robin's plantain, and different types of trillium. Just look where the dogs are sniffing—they will usually lead you to the flowers.

The trail hugs dry, sunny hillsides, which is good habitat for many wildflowers. Flowering dogwood trees will be blooming in spring, amid a forest of pine, hemlock, rhododendron, and mountain laurel. In early spring, the hardwoods will not yet have their leaves, so as the trail climbs higher, views of the rough-and-tumble Green River appear through the trees.

At 1 mile cross Pulliam Creek again—a good spot for dogs to take a drink before starting a steep climb. The length of the hike and the steepness of this part of the trail, especially in warmer months, will make people and dogs extra thirsty. Bring plenty of drinking water for everyone.

At about 2 miles a narrow trail sharply descends to the Green River Narrows, a dangerous section of rapids on the river. Do not take this trail. It is extremely steep, not maintained, and even if you are an adept climber, your dog probably will have great difficulty.

Instead, continue on the trail and at just over 2 miles, you will come to a sign for the Green River Cove Trail. Turn right here and take this trail to descend about 0.75 mile to the Green River. This is, for some, the highlight of the hike, where courageous kayakers can be seen shooting through the narrow, treacherous stretch of rapids. Some large boulders perched out in a section of the river before reaching the narrows provide a great place for lunch and kayak watching.

Plenty of shallow pools wait between the rocks for dogs to drink, splash around in, and cool off, but hold on to them and watch them closely. If they get too far out into the river, the quick current would be too much for them to swim across safely.

After sufficient resting and river viewing, backtrack up the Green River Cove Trail to the Pulliam Creek Trail and back to the parking area.

A bloodroot flower—one of the first spring arrivals—blooms along the Pulliam Creek Trail in the Green River Game Lands.

27. Pine Tree Loop Trail—Bent Creek Experimental Forest

Loop: 2 miles
Hiking time: 1 hour
Best time to hike: Year-round
High point: 2400 feet
Elevation gain: 270 feet
Difficulty: Easy
Rules and fees: Dogs must be on a leash, except during fall hunting season
Maps: USGS Dunsmore Mountain; Bent Creek Trail
Contact: Bent Creek Experimental Forest, 828-667-5261; Pisgah Ranger District, Pisgah National Forest, 828-877-3265; *www.cs.unca.edu/nfsnc*

Getting there: Take Interstate 26 east to exit 33/Blue Ridge Parkway. Turn left onto NC 191/Brevard Road and drive 2 miles. Turn right at the light on Bent Creek Ranch Road, and bear left onto Wesley Branch Road. Go about 2 miles and pull into the Hard Times trailhead parking area on the left to access the trail. Another parking area is at the Lake Powhatan Campground, about 0.3 mile farther down Wesley Branch Road, but a day use fee is assessed there.

The Bent Creek area, just a few miles south of Asheville, is known as an experimental forest, established in 1925 by the U.S. Forest Service to conduct research on forest management and the ecology of the southern Appalachians. Amid the scientific research, outdoor recreation is allowed and encouraged in this 6000-acre forest, brimming with wooded trails, single-track terrain, rivers, and a lake. This makes Bent Creek (which also borders the North Carolina Arboretum), the definitive multiuse area, attracting people who come to hike, mountain bike, trail run, fish, hunt, swim, ride horses, camp, picnic, and walk their dogs.

At times, especially in summer and fall, the area can be congested, but if you hike during the off-season or on a weekday, it is a perfect

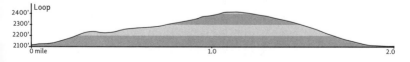

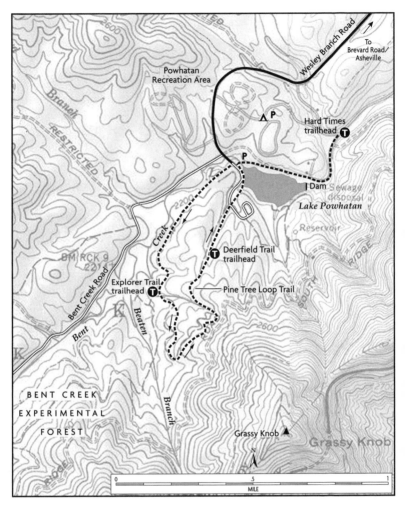

place to hike with your dog. If hiking during fall hunting season (in North Carolina, hunting seasons run from September to May), place a blaze orange vest on your dog, since hunting is permitted in the national forest. Currently, hunting is prohibited on Sundays throughout the state.

The Pine Tree Loop Trail is one of many great little hikes in the Bent Creek area, winding through forests and fields and crossing enough streams to keep dogs interested, alert, and happy. Although mountain bikes are allowed on this trail, it is flat and wide enough for users to safely pass each other. Bikes are supposed to yield to hikers, but to protect yourself and your dog, play it safe and step out of the way if you see a bike approaching. The trail is closed to horses.

If you are camping in the Lake Powhatan Campground, open from April through October, the trailhead is easily accessible from the campsites. From the Hard Times trailhead, walk behind the locked gate and follow the wide, level road for 0.3 mile. At the crossroads, turn right and walk about 0.2 mile with Bent Creek on your left.

You will soon hear rushing water and see it spilling over the dam on the left, then come to Lake Powhatan. During the appropriate season, the lake is open for fishing and swimming, but dogs are not allowed to swim there. Continue to walk around the lake to the northwest, turning left on a path blazed yellow and walk across the footbridge. On the other side, turn right onto the road and in a few seconds arrive at the trail sign for the Pine Tree Loop Trail on the left.

Jon and his chocolate Lab, Talley, take time out for bonding and picture taking on the trail.

Follow the blue-blazed trail into the gently rising forest, with a small stream running along the right. What makes this an enjoyable hike for people are the interpretive signs, which tell the story of the trail and the forest, such as the first sign, "Natural Disturbances." It explains the appearance of the large, uprooted trees visible on the trailside, the handiwork of Hurricane Opal in 1995.

Another sign, about 0.5 mile farther along, "Laurel and Rhododendron," explains the importance of these shrublike thickets of trees, found so abundantly throughout western North Carolina, providing protective cover for many wildlife species, and helping to control soil erosion. In spring, the trees also provide lovely, showy white flowers.

At 1 mile, the trail comes upon an open field briefly before heading back into the woods. Soon come to an intersection with the Explorer Trail to the right. The Pine Tree Trail continues to the left, near the "Mountain Settlement" interpretive sign, which tells the story of the old homesteaders who lived in the area. A few hundred feet off the trail behind the sign are the remains of a stone fireplace.

Heading northeast, continue to another trail intersection. The yellow-blazed Deerfield Trail goes to the right. Bear left to stay on the Pine Tree Loop Trail and soon come to a gravel road. Turn left to see Lake Powhatan on the right. Cross the bridge to the right and backtrack to the parking area.

28. Carolina Mountain Trail— The North Carolina Arboretum

Loop: 2.4 miles
Hiking time: 1 hour
Best time to hike: Year-round
High point: 2200 feet
Elevation gain: 150 feet
Difficulty: Easy
Rules and fees: Dogs are allowed on trails only and must be on a leash; daily parking fee but free on Tuesdays
Maps: USGS Skyland; The North Carolina Arboretum
Contact: North Carolina Arboretum, 828-665-2492; *www.ncarboretum.org*

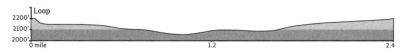

Getting there: Take Interstate 26 to exit 33/Brevard Road/NC 191. Turn south onto Brevard Road/NC 191 and drive 2.5 miles. Turn right at the light for the Blue Ridge Parkway/North Carolina Arboretum entrance and bear right into the arboretum. Do not get on the Blue Ridge Parkway. After the gatehouse, drive 1 mile toward the education center. Park in the main parking area, walk south toward the education center, and look for the trailhead sign.

The North Carolina Arboretum is so much more than a typical public garden. Established in 1986 as an affiliate of the University of North Carolina, the arboretum is a center for education, research, conservation, economic development, and garden demonstration. The 434-acre outdoor wonderland contains elaborately planned and manicured gardens and greenhouses, but it also sits within the Bent Creek Experimental Forest of the Pisgah National Forest, just a few miles south of Asheville, and has miles of woodland trails, which are also meticulously maintained.

The arboretum trails offer a lovely hiking experience for those people and their dogs looking for more of a casual walk through the woods than a rugged mountain adventure. Several short trails are rated from easy to difficult by the arboretum staff. The Carolina Mountain Trail is considered easy and is suitable for dogs in any season. It starts behind the Education Center, a great starting point for gathering information on the trails, gardens, trees, flowers, birds, and other local wildlife. The center also has restrooms and a small café, but dogs are not allowed inside the building.

The Carolina Mountain Trail is blazed with a green circle and a hiker, denoting it is only for foot traffic. Descend a set of stairs into a pine and mixed hardwood forest. At the first 0.1 mile come to a road. Cross a wooden bridge—easy access here for dogs to wet their paws and take a sip of stream water—and continue on the wide, easy, woodchip path lined with holly and pine trees. After another 0.1 mile the Greenhouse is visible to the right, and a sign directs you to keep going for another 0.3 mile to a connector trail to the Greenhouse.

Continue on the Carolina Mountain Trail, pass one of several log benches along this trail, and soon hear Bent Creek gurgling in the distance. At the top of a short set of ascending stairs you will see a sign pointing right toward the Greenhouse 0.1 mile away, but bear left to continue on the Carolina Mountain Trail, soon arriving at Wolf Branch Road. Head directly across the road and descend stairs entering into a dense rhododendron grove. Tightly knit trees with low-hanging branches form a snug little tunnel and an idyllic setting as the trail passes along the creek. Mini waterfalls and log benches complete the picture.

You will want to linger a while, and so will the dogs. The stream is shallow and narrow enough in this little hideaway for bigger dogs to wade across, splash around, and have a drink. The path through the tunnels only lasts about 0.2 mile.

At just over 1 mile from the start, you will exit the rhododendron grove and come to Bent Creek Road. To the immediate right is a gate behind which stretches the Bent Creek Experimental Forest and the road to Lake Powhatan. This is technically the end of the Carolina Mountain Trail, so at this juncture you have three options for returning to the trailhead: (1) create a loop trail by turning left on the road for the Bent Creek Trail, a blue-blazed trail that weaves in and out of the woods and crisscrosses Bent Creek Road along Bent Creek to the Education Center; (2) create a loop by staying on Bent Creek Road, a wide, flat, dirt-and-gravel road shared with walkers, runners, and bicyclists; or (3) turn back into the rhododendron grove and retrace your steps on the Carolina Mountain Trail to the trailhead. All options are just a little over 1 mile long.

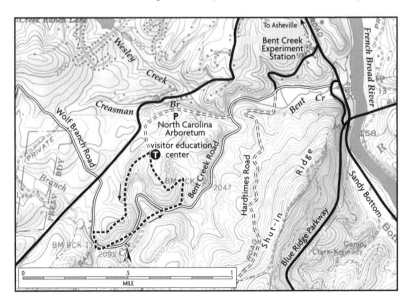

The trails in the North Carolina Arboretum are well marked and well maintained.

If you decide to take the Bent Creek Trail or Bent Creek Road, head east, and when you come to a stone-sided bridge over Bent Creek, bear left on Bent Creek Road. From here, it is about 0.5 mile to the intersection with Running Cedar Road. Turn left here and begin a slightly steep ascent. Continue 0.5 mile to the gardens and the Education Center.

29. Max Patch Trail

Loop: 3.5 miles
Hiking time: 2 hours
Best time to hike: Year-round
High point: 4629 feet
Elevation gain: 429 feet
Difficulty: Moderate
Rules and fees: Dogs must be on a leash
Maps: USGS Lemon Gap; U.S. Forest Service Harmon Den and Hot Springs Area of the Pisgah National Forest
Contact: Appalachian Ranger District, Pisgah National Forest, 828-622-3202; *www.cs.unca.edu/nfsnc*

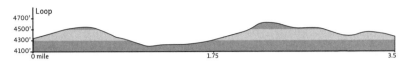

Getting there: Take Interstate 40 west to exit 7/Harmon Den. Veer right onto Cold Springs Road (Forest Service Road 148), which is unpaved, and drive for 6.2 miles. Turn left onto Max Patch Road (Forest Service Road 1182), also unpaved, and drive for 1.9 miles to the Max Patch parking area on the right.

If Max Patch (4629 feet elevation) is not the ultimate hiking destination for dogs, then it comes pretty close. One of the obvious signs is that just about every other hiker comes to the mountain with her dog. And this is not an easy place to reach. Deep in the Harmon Den area of the Pisgah National Forest near the Tennessee border, the only direct access is on miles of unpaved Forest Service roads. Yet on any given weekend throughout the year, the dirt trailhead parking area is filled to overflowing, a testament to the alluring, unique beauty of Max Patch.

Many trails crisscross the area, including the nearly 2200-mile-long Appalachian Trail, which cuts a northeast path across the Max Patch summit. The most popular day hikes are two loop trails. The longer, 2.4-mile loop circles the base of the mountain. The smaller, 1.4-mile loop crosses the summit. Each loop can be hiked separately as complete loops for a total 3.8-mile workout, or they can be combined for a 3.5-mile hike (because the trails overlap a bit), which is the hike described here.

Start the trail by going around the gate, past the signboard, and heading up the left route on the Max Patch Trail. You will see the giant bald—a grassy, treeless mountain summit—directly ahead, with the tiny dots of hikers circling the top. In the 1800s, the mountain was cleared as pastureland for cows and sheep, and the Forest Service maintains the grassy knob with the use of periodic mowing and prescribed burns.

The path to the top is wide and grassy with easy footing but steady climbing. The rippling mountain views from every step are incredible, so plan this trip on a clear day. In spring, wildflowers are abundant, including trilliums, violets, and bluets along the trail edges. You will have to tug on leashes frequently to get your dogs' noses out of the grasses. Fall is an especially beautiful time to hike, but it is also hunting season. Although walking across Max Patch, out in the open, is not dangerous, dogs should wear a blaze orange vest when venturing into the woods.

At 0.5 mile, top out at a meadow area with an altitude of about 4550 feet, and soon after come to a trailhead sign pointing right for the summit in 0.1 mile, and left for the long loop around in 1.9 miles. Head to the left, following wooden posts with the white rectangular blazes of the Appalachian Trail (AT). Descend slightly and enter a dense forest of oaks, maples, and hemlocks. Campsites are scattered through the forest—keep a close watch for the white blazes to stay on track.

Arrive at a thick tunnel of rhododendron at about 1 mile and a little spring running across the trail, the only water source you might encounter on the trail. Walk along a wooden fence and come to a campsite, behind which sits a wide meadow. Veer around to the left, and at 1.25

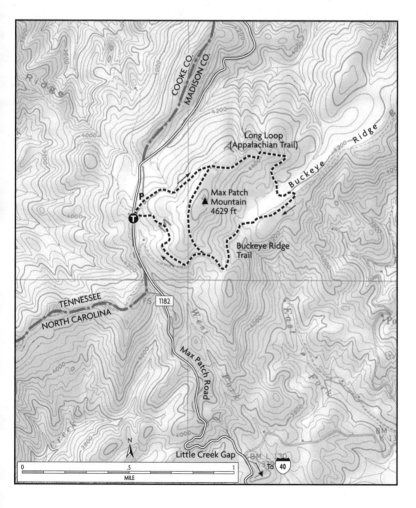

Relaxing on Max Patch bald

miles come to a fork. The AT turns left here, passing on to Lemon Gap in 4.6 miles. Turn right to continue the loop back to the Max Patch Trail via Buckeye Ridge. At 1.45 miles arrive at another fork and continue straight on the Buckeye Ridge Trail. Even though you are below the summit, the views are beautiful.

At 1.75 miles, come to a fork. The Buckeye Ridge Trail and the AT continue to the left. Turn right here to continue on the Max Patch Trail to the summit. At 2 miles, the wide trail continues straight, while the Max Patch Trail branches off to the right. Turn here and almost immediately turn right again for the summit. Start ascending some steps before hitting a narrow dirt trail along the back side of the mountain. The stunning views of rippling mountains, meadows, and fields interspersed with forest seem to stretch endlessly.

When you arrive at the bald summit, it is a Maria von Trapp moment, and you will almost want to start singing. Continue on the trail, following white markers, and find a place to spread a blanket and a picnic. Some people even bring lawn chairs, taking the short way up and spending the day. Be sure to bring treats and water for the dogs, since you will want to linger here for a long while.

When it is time to go, backtrack down the back side of the mountain, turning right at the fork, and walk along the ridge to return to the parking area.

30. Lovers Leap Loop Trail

Round-trip: 1.6 miles
Hiking time: 1 hour
Best time to hike: Spring through fall
High point: 1810 feet
Elevation gain: 510 feet
Difficulty: Strenuous
Rules and fees: Dogs must be on a leash
Maps: USGS Hot Springs; U.S. Forest Service Harmon Den and Hot
   Springs Area
Contact: Appalachian Ranger District, Pisgah National Forest,
   828-622-3202; *www.cs.unca.edu/nfsnc*

Getting there: From Hot Springs in Madison County, take US 25/70 east across the French Broad River Bridge. Immediately after crossing the bridge, turn left onto SR 1304/River Road. Turn left at the first intersection and follow the road around to the left, past the rafting access area, through a residential neighborhood, to the Silvermine trailhead parking area.

To reach the Lovers Leap Trail, you first need to hike a portion of the Appalachian Trail—probably the country's most famous long-distance trail, starting in Georgia and ending 2176 miles later in Maine—which

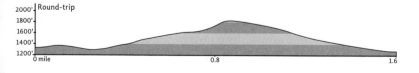

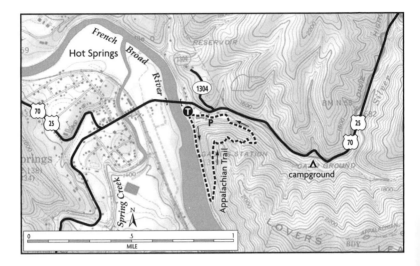

runs right through the town of Hot Springs. From the parking area, walk back along the road you just drove in on and turn left at the Silvermine trailhead, following the Appalachian Trail's white rectangular blazes. The Lovers Leap Trail intersects with the Appalachian Trail after about 0.5 mile.

The whole loop is a treat to hike with different features offered at every turn, but this first section might be the most enjoyable for dogs. Lined in shady maples, oaks, river birches, sourwoods, and tulip poplars, the trail runs right along the French Broad River. The view of the river is so pretty you might forget to watch your footing, but the trail is rocky and uneven in places. The walking gets more difficult and strenuous, so be sure your dog is a nimble, energetic hiker before starting out.

At just over 0.1 mile, a little spur trail on the right leads down to the water by a small cascade that stretches all the way across the river. There are many other easy access points, where dogs will no doubt stop for a splash or a drink.

At 0.3 mile, the trail veers to the left and starts climbing steeply over rocky terrain. Continue ascending switchbacks, passing among pine trees as the trail hugs the mountainside. The climbing is arduous, but the views just keep getting better and better as you climb higher above the river.

At 0.5 mile come to the first of several overlooks on the large rock outcrop known as Lovers Leap Ridge, which takes its name from a Cherokee Indian legend about a heartbroken young man who flung himself from this 500-foot precipice. Try not to think of that while enjoying the views of the French Broad River valley and the town of Hot Springs, framed here in large oak and pine trees. The sweeping views are awesome at any time of year, but in fall, when the leaves turn the mountains to red and gold, the scenery is spectacular. However, the drop-offs are steep, and the loose, rocky soil around the overlooks can be slippery, so if you have a wayward or wandering type of dog, now is a good time to have him on a leash.

Continue climbing and admiring the scenery and soon come to the intersection with the Lovers Leap Loop Trail. The trailhead sign points right to continue the Appalachian Trail or left for the Lovers Leap and

Dawn, with Noah catching a ride in a baby backpack, checks out the sights of the forest.

Silvermine trails. Take the left fork and enter a dense rhododendron grove. The trail is supposedly marked with orange blazes. Though the blazes are hard to spot, the trail is well used.

Begin a very steep descent over a narrow, hard-packed trail. The footing is easier here since it is not as rocky as the uphill portion, but mounds of dry leaves on the ground in late autumn can make it slippery.

At about 1.4 miles you will arrive at a fork with the Pump Gap Trail, which continues straight ahead for a 4.2-mile loop. Turn left here to continue on the Lovers Leap Trail, and descend into a damp, boulder-strewn area running along a creek. Follow this trail out to the Silvermine trailhead parking area.

31. Laurel River Trail

Round-trip: 7 miles
Hiking time: 3.5 hours
Best time to hike: Year-round
High point: 1630 feet
Elevation gain: 220 feet
Difficulty: Moderate
Rules and fees: Dogs must be on a leash
Maps: USGS Hot Springs; U.S. Forest Service Harmon Den and Hot Springs Area
Contact: Appalachian Ranger District, Pisgah National Forest, 828-622-3202; *www.cs.unca.edu/nfsnc*

Getting there: From Hot Springs, take US 25/70 east to the intersection with SR 208 at Big Laurel Creek. Turn right (US 25/70) and park about 100 yards down on the right in a dirt parking area. The trailhead is at the end of the parking area at the Forest Service sign.

For dogs who love the woods and love the water, this trail is as good as it gets. Laurel River is also one of the flattest trails to be found in the mountain region of western North Carolina, making the 7-mile out-and-back trail seem like a cakewalk.

The Laurel River Trail (which actually runs along Big Laurel Creek) is a great hike in spring for wildflower enthusiasts, as well as a great trail in summer because of its heavy shade and places to cool off in the river, while

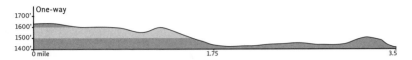

fall is spectacular with colorful leaves and late-blooming wildflowers. The relatively low elevation and the shelter from wind by protective cliff faces and trees also make this a mild hike during winter.

Start at the end of the parking area by the trailhead sign for the Laurel River Trail, which is also open to mountain bikes. Enter a narrow trail lined in hemlock and mountain laurel running right along the creek, where you are likely to spot trout fishermen and the occasional kayaker. Almost immediately the trail splits—the right fork slopes down to the creek but rejoins the main trail in a few moments. At 0.2 mile, pass a gravel road that enters from the left. Continue straight, and pass through a section of private property—be sure to keep dogs on a leash and on the gravel road.

Start to walk along a high cliff face on the left side of the trail, with wildflowers such as orange touch-me-nots, goldenrod, and aster growing in shadow in early fall, with the gentle rapids of the river rushing to your right. In 0.7 mile, arrive at another fork and stay to the right. It would be hard to get off trail, but you will see intermittent, and very faded, yellow blazes. Just stick close to the creek and you should be fine.

The trail is often damp and muddy, being so close to the river. Waterproof shoes come in handy. At 1.5 miles, arrive at a little beach area to the right, with easy access by way of boulder hopping to get out into the river. It is a good place for a picnic or a snack, and for dogs to take a swim, but be careful of the swift-flowing currents.

Back on the trail, it starts to get rockier, with big slabs of chunky rocks that can be slippery after a rain. The trail then smooths out again, with easier footing beneath a fluffy canopy of hemlock, mountain laurel, maple, and oak and lovely little cascades and ripples down in the creek. At just over 2 miles, the trail and river squeeze into a narrow gorge with high, jagged rock walls that make for louder and livelier river rapids.

At a little over 2.5 miles, start veering away from the river where the trees give way to a thick undergrowth of grasses and bushes. To the left you will pass some seemingly out-of-place concrete remnants of an old sawmill that operated here at the turn of the twentieth century but closed in 1927. A town of 1000 people once lived here, but all that is left is known as the "ghost town" of Runion.

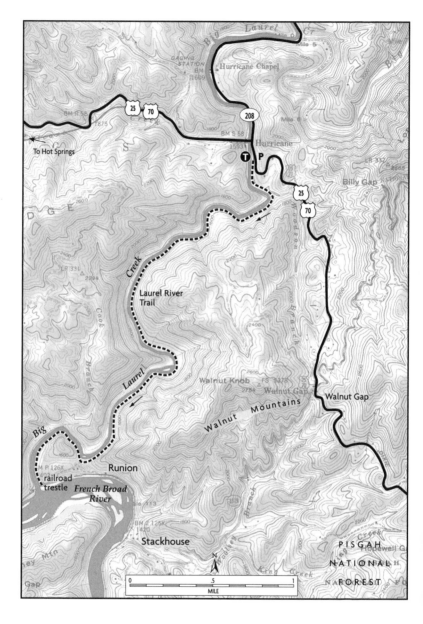

At 3.5 miles, arrive at a railroad trestle and tracks. You can turn back here, or climb up and over a steep, gravel incline and cross over to the other side of the tracks. Descend into woods again for about 250 feet to a beach area and the confluence with the French Broad River—a popular

river for kayakers and rafters. A campsite sits back in the woods against a small beach area, where thin-leaved sunflowers and pretty red cardinal flowers grow. This is a nice calm spot for the dogs to take a swim and snack before backtracking.

Pat and Sammy hike on the Laurel River Trail, which runs along Big Laurel Creek.

32. High Bluff and Rhododendron Gardens Trails—Roan Mountain

Round-trip: 3.5 miles
Hiking time: 1.5 hours
Best time to hike: April through November
High point: 6200 feet
Elevation gain: 100 feet
Difficulty: Moderate
Rules and fees: Dogs do not need to be on a leash on trails, except in the developed areas, parking lots, and picnic areas; they must be under voice control at all times; small parking fee
Map: USGS Bakersville
Contact: Toecane Ranger District, Pisgah National Forest, 828-682-6146; *www.cs.unca.edu/nfsnc*

Getting there: From Bakersville, drive about 13 miles north on NC 261 to Carvers Gap and turn left at the Roan Mountain Forest Service sign and a parking area. Continue another 1.6 miles to a gatehouse. This road is open from April through November. There is a small fee to park here. Once past the gatehouse, turn to the paved parking area on the right.

Since the road up to the Roan Mountain Rhododendron Gardens is only open April through November, there is limited time to hike here. The best time to visit has an even smaller window—during the Catawba rhododendron blooms. The bright, fluffy pinkish-purple flowers of these evergreen trees usually reach their peak bloom from mid- to late-June and are not to be missed if hiking in this high-country region of western North Carolina. Several hiking options range from the strenuous trek across the heath balds of the Appalachian Trail to Roan High Knob, to a short jaunt to Roan High Bluff with a side loop through the Rhododendron Gardens, which is the hike described here.

Start the Roan High Bluff and Rhododendron Gardens trails at the near side of the parking area—restrooms are at the far end, near the site of the old Cloudland Hotel. The trail enters a cool forest of tall spruce, pine, and Fraser fir on a path of soft soil welcoming to little paws. In about 100 feet, come to a fork. Stay to the left. At 0.2 mile, the Rhododendron Gardens Trail branches off to the left, which you will take on the return. For now, continue straight to reach Roan High Bluff.

At 0.3 mile, come to another fork and turn right. In spring the edges of the trail are thickly lined with ferns, yarrow, periwinkle-colored bluets, and other wildflowers. Overhead and on all sides, the Catawba rhododendron grow in profusion, large, deep pink, and picturesque.

Catawba rhododendron blooms

At about 0.45 mile, climb up wood steps and cross a dirt road to continue on the trail. At 0.5 mile, emerge at a parking area. If you have a curious dog prone to running and wandering, now is a good time to put him on a leash, especially as you arrive at the popular picnic area.

Continue up a paved path and begin a steep ascent to the overlook. About 20 minutes and 1.2 miles from the trailhead, reach Roan High Bluff with a wooden platform overlook, at 6200 feet elevation. An interpretive sign describes the cliff area as "One of the rarest communities in the Southern Appalachians. . . . It contains 288 plant species of which 18 live only on high rock outcroppings."

The views from this vantage are awesome when the fog lifts, but the conditions are often chilly and windy. You can rest for a moment on some large boulders and give yourself and the dog some water after the climb. It can get crowded on the trail and the overlook on weekends, especially during bloom season, so if you crave more elbow room, hike this trail during the week or very early in the day.

Backtrack to the sign for the Rhododendron Gardens Trail. Turn right here and come to another parking lot. Walk past the picnic area toward

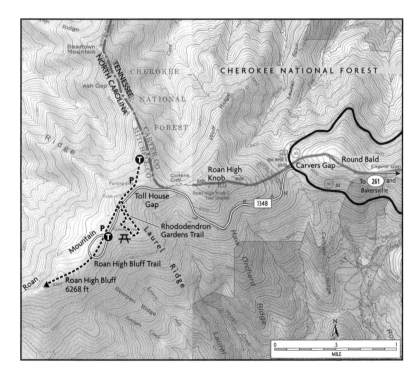

The fluffy, pink blooms of the Catawba Rhododendron are a highlight of a hike to the Roan Mountain area in June.

the restrooms and an information cabin, which is open daily Memorial Day through Labor Day and five days a week in September and October. The Rhododendron Gardens Trail starts to the right of the cabin on a paved, figure-eight trail with numbered signs that correspond to a self-guiding booklet available at the trailhead. Benches are scattered throughout and rhododendron blooms are everywhere.

The booklet leads you along a series of numbered posts that describe the natural history of this Canada-like environment. An observation deck that lies halfway around the first, paved portion of the loop trail looks over the Black Mountains on a clear day to Mount Mitchell (the highest peak in the East). Directly in front and below the platform you can see why this is called a "garden"—a thick carpet of rhododendron appears to be growing well-manicured under the hand of an artful gardener. Continue on the paved path, which leads back to the information cabin. Cross back over the parking lot to the woods and turn right on the trail, back to the original trailhead.

WESTERN PIEDMONT/ FOOTHILLS REGION

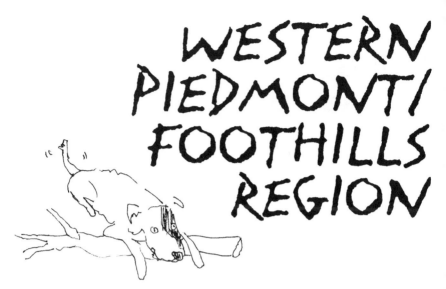

33. Sandy Cliff Overlook and Lake Channel Overlook Trails —Lake James State Park

Round-trip: 2 miles
Hiking time: 45 minutes
Best time to hike: Year-round
High point: 1280 feet
Elevation gain: 80 feet
Difficulty: Easy
Rules and fees: Dogs must be on a leash no longer than 6 feet
Maps: USGS Marion East; Lake James State Park
Contact: Lake James State Park, 828-652-5047; *www.ncparks.gov*

Getting there: Lake James State Park is about 5 miles northeast of Marion on NC 126. Take Interstate 40 to exit 90/Nebo/Lake James and head north. Go 0.5 mile and turn right onto Harmony Grove Road. Drive for 2 miles to a stoplight. Go straight across the intersection and past Nebo Elementary School to a stop sign. Turn right onto NC 126, and follow the signs to the park entrance 2.3 miles on the left. Follow the road to the parking area at the park office.

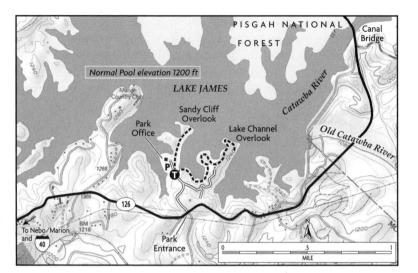

Lake James is such a gem of a park in this part of the state that visiting is a must on your dog's hiking list. With only four designated trails in the park, and none difficult, Lake James is not the place for an energy-packed workout but rather for a quick, low-stress hike through beautiful country with your dog. Since the focal point at this park is the lake, most visitors come to swim, fish, boat, and picnic, and you are very likely to have the trails all to yourself.

To get the best views of Lake James, combine the Sandy Cliff Overlook Trail (0.5 mile round-trip) with the Lake Channel Overlook Trail (1.5 miles round-trip) for a 45-minute to 1-hour hike.

Start the Sandy Cliff Overlook Trail by heading back a bit along the edge of the picnic area toward the park entrance. Follow the white circle blaze through an entryway of towering pine trees on a paved path that quickly turns to dirt and gravel. The trailhead for the Lake Channel Overlook Trail will be on the right, but continue past the sign for now.

The lake is visible on both sides of the trail, which is lined in pine, oak, maple, mountain laurel, and rhododendron. Spring is a fun time for dogs (and people), when wildflowers such as violets and daisies start to pop up on the trail edges.

The trail ends at the Sandy Cliff Overlook platform with a bench perched perfectly in a shady spot to view the expansive lake. Straight across Lake James is 3127-foot-high Shortoff Mountain, hovering to the right of the Linville Gorge Wilderness Area, part of the Pisgah National Forest.

The lake, which was named for James B. Duke, founder of the Duke Power Company, was created between 1916 and 1923 with the construction of dams across the Catawba River and two tributaries—Paddy Creek and the Linville River. Two lakes were formed, then connected by a canal to form Lake James, with 150 miles of shoreline. Since it was formed, the lake has been part of a hydroelectric unit for the power company.

Dogs will not care about the lake's history but will likely be mesmerized by the sights and sounds of boats zipping by on the glasslike lake surface. The humans on the hike will drink in the picture-perfect landscape (get a look quick—the pretty, pine tree–lined shoreline is quickly disappearing to home developments).

Backtrack nearly 0.25 mile, turning left at the Lake Channel Overlook sign and taking the red diamond–blazed trail hugging the lake. Many small critters, such as red and gray foxes, squirrels, and rabbits, roam

The view from Sandy Cliff Overlook stretches across Lake James to the Linville Gorge Wilderness.

the woods, dominated by hemlock and pine and mixed hardwoods. The lake also has its share of wildlife, including mallards, great blue herons, green herons, and Canada geese. If your dog has a propensity for chasing waterfowl, hang on tight to the leash. The lure of these birds, as well as the water, is often unavoidable for dogs, but be sure not to let them swim off and possibly come into contact with speedboats.

About 0.3 mile from the Lake Channel Overlook trailhead, cross a footbridge by a boat ramp. Turn right to stay on the Lake Channel Trail, heading uphill. Soon turn left onto a road, then right at the overlook sign, ascending a set of stairs to a bathroom and parking area. Bear left and follow the trail signs. Walk along a road lined in dogwood trees, whose white flowers start to bloom in April.

At about 0.8 mile, arrive at the Lake Channel Overlook, another perfect, pine-shaded wooden platform with benches from which you will find it hard to leave. The overlook is just southeast from the Sandy Cliff Overlook, so the views are similar, peering across the crystal blue water to the Linville Gorge Wilderness Area and Shortoff Mountain. A variety of boats entertain as they either speed, chug, or float by on the lake, about 90 feet below.

This spot is as good as any to have a small picnic (there are no garbage cans at the overlook, though, so pack out what you pack in), before backtracking to the parking area.

34. Shinny and Upper Falls Trails—South Mountains State Park

Loop: 7.4 miles
Hiking time: 4 hours
Best time to hike: Year-round
High point: 2250 feet
Elevation gain: 895 feet
Difficulty: Strenuous
Rules and fees: Dogs must be on a leash no longer than 6 feet
Maps: USGS Benn Knob; South Mountains State Park
Contact: South Mountains State Park, 828-433-4772; *www .ncparks.gov*

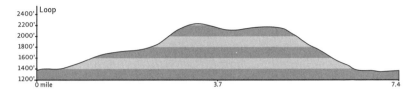

Getting there: From Interstate 40, take exit 105 and turn south on NC 18. Travel 11.1 miles, and turn right onto SR 1913 (Sugarloaf Road). Take SR 1913 for 4.3 miles to Old NC 18 and turn left. Drive 2.7 miles and turn right onto SR 1901 (Wards Gap Road). The park is 1.4 miles off SR 1901 on SR 1904 (South Mountains Park Avenue). Travel 1 mile to the South Mountains State Park gate. Once in the park, drive to the Jacob Fork parking area.

A good way to see a large portion of the sprawling 18,000 acres of South Mountains State Park in Burke County is to combine several trails to form a 7.4-mile loop. You and the dogs will get to climb rugged mountain terrain, cool your paws by fording streams, enjoy the diversity of flowers, trees, and geologic formations, and catch the foaming spray of a massive waterfall.

Start out on the Headquarters Trail by walking through the Jacob Fork River picnic area. Pass the restrooms and continue to a gravel road parallel to the rushing Jacob Fork River. Head west on the road shaded by large hemlocks, and at 0.2 mile pass the Chestnut Knob trailhead on the right, a strenuous 2-mile hike to an overlook. Stay on the road and soon come to a bridge over Shinny Creek. Pronounced "shiny," the waterway is named for the shiny flecks of mica that sparkle on the ground.

Pass the Shinny Creek picnic area and come to a fork with a sign for High Shoals to the left and Shinny Creek Campground to the right. Go right and start climbing a dirt-and-gravel trail lined in hemlock and holly with the creek now running on the right.

The path is wide, steep, and gravelly—the large rock chunks might be hard on soft paw pads. Keep climbing among oak, maple, hickory, and poplar trees.

At just over 1 mile, come to Shinny Creek Campground on the left. If you continue straight across the bridge on the Headquarters Trail, it will take you in a shorter loop back to High Shoals Falls and the parking area. If the dogs are trail-hardy and up for a challenge, take the trail to the right, the "Shinny Trail to Possum Trail," and enter a soft-floored forest.

This trail becomes a backwoods adventure with water-warped and precariously narrow log footbridges—or stream crossings with no bridges at all. One such place soon appears. With no bridge at this Shinny Creek crossing, you will need to do some serious rock hopping. You will get wet—water is knee deep in places, especially after a rain. Water-loving dogs should have no problem wading and swimming across.

At about 1.5 miles, come to a sign pointing right to the Possum Trail. Stay straight ahead on the Shinny Trail, walking among a sea of rhododendron, and soon arrive at another bridgeless stream crossing. Dogs will love the chance to dip in the creek, but be careful of the quick current.

Keep climbing and winding through the woods, ascending through a mixed conifer and hardwood forest to a ridge top at an altitude of about 1880 feet. The constant uphill can take a toll on dogs during warm weather. Be sure to bring extra drinking water, and consider hiking here during fall.

The trail continues to dip and climb as you hike in a northwesterly direction and then heads south after about 3.5 miles. Continue hiking south for about another mile until you come to a junction with the Headquarters Trail. Turn to the left, heading back east toward the Upper Falls Trail. After about 1 mile, come to a fork with the Headquarters Trail looping back to the left. Continue straight (east) on the Upper Falls Trail for nearly another mile to the junction near the Upper Falls area. This is most likely the only area in the park where you will encounter trail traffic.

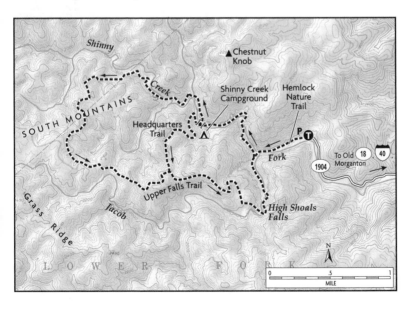

High Shoals Falls plunges 80 feet, creating a wide spray, along the Upper Falls Trail.

A trailhead sign directs you right for High Shoals Falls—a spectacular waterfall that plunges some 80 feet into a deep pool. While the scenery is great, the extremely steep descending stairs can be difficult to navigate with a large dog, especially on weekends with a lot of visitors. The trail to the left leads to the parking area if you feel the need to avoid the falls.

At the next fork, turn left for the falls, cross a boardwalk over the falls, and start to descend a series of many steep steps to the next viewing area, where you and the dogs can cool off in the soaking spray of the falls. Continue the steep descent from here over slippery rocks. Back at the gravel road leading to the parking area, veer to the right to take the last 0.75 mile on the Hemlock Nature Trail, which offers a self-guided nature walk through interpretive signs as it hugs the Jacob Fork River.

35. Pinnacle Trail—Crowders Mountain State Park

Loop: 3.4 miles

Hiking time: 2 hours

Best time to hike: Year-round

High point: 1705 feet

Elevation gain: 850

Difficulty: Strenuous

Rules and fees: Dogs must be on a 6-foot leash and attended at all times

Maps: USGS Kings Mountain; Crowders Mountain State Park

Contact: Crowders Mountain State Park, 704-853-5375; *www .ncparks.gov*

Getting there: Heading south, take Interstate 85 to exit 13 to Edgewood Road. At the top of the ramp turn left onto Edgewood Road. At the first stoplight, turn right onto Franklin Boulevard/US 74 and drive about 2 miles. At the second stoplight, turn left onto Sparrow Springs Road.

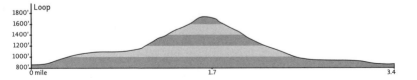

Continue on Sparrow Springs Road for about 2 miles, and turn right to continue on Sparrow Springs Road. The main entrance to the park will be on the right in less than 1 mile.

Crowders Mountain State Park is a dog's mecca. Located so closely to Charlotte, the state's largest city, the park offers a green oasis, a much-needed forest setting for city dwellers—both the human and canine kind. On any given weekend during the year the many wooded park trails are filled with hikers and their dogs getting a bit of fresh air, mountain

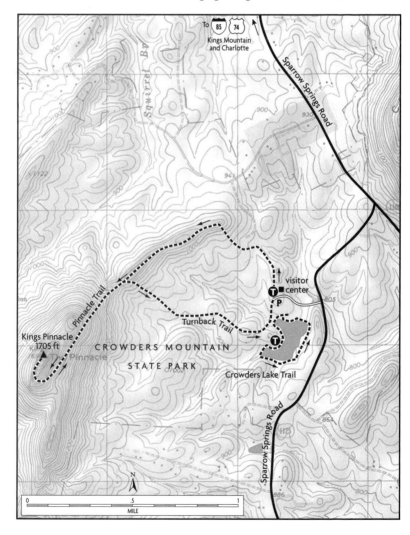

Small dogs, such as this little pug named Gus, will have to be carried up to the summit on Pinnacle Trail.

scenery, and outdoor exercise. Sitting in the state's foothills, at the edge of the western mountain region, the entrance to Crowders Mountain State Park sits at an altitude of about 900 feet, but its trails climb to commanding viewpoints of nearly 2000 feet. Since it is so close to the South Carolina border, the park has temperate weather for hiking through fall, winter, and spring, but summer is usually too warm for large-breed or long-haired dogs.

The Pinnacle Trail is one of the park's more difficult trails due to its elevation gain—more than 800 feet in less than 2 miles, about 600 feet of which take place in about the last third of the climb up. But the trail takes you to Kings Pinnacle (1705 feet), the higher of the two peaks in the park (the other is Crowders Mountain) with sweeping views of the surrounding valleys and the cities of Charlotte and Kings Mountain. This trail is only for the hardiest dogs and is better suited for small dogs that can be lifted over a large boulder just below the summit. Large dogs will have a difficult time scrambling up this rock. Other trails in Crowders Mountain State Park (Hikes 36 and 37) are better for larger dogs.

Start the trail behind the park office, heading north on the wide Pinnacle Trail blazed with an orange circle and lined in tall oaks and white pines. At 0.5 mile the gently winding trail starts to gradually ascend and will shortly become rockier and narrower. At about 1 mile come to an intersection with the Turnback Trail, which veers to the left with a white triangular blaze. This is an alternative route back to the parking area for those people or dogs who are not up for the steep climb ahead. If you have enough energy and water—there are no creeks or other water sources on this trail—continue on the Pinnacle Trail.

The trail starts filling with rocks and boulders until you are rock climbing more than hiking. Progress is slow and footing a bit challenging through this rock garden, as the trail weaves through evergreen branches. This is a place where dogs seem to have an easier time maneuvering than humans.

Ducks will mesmerize dogs on the Crowders Lake Trail, located near the trailhead for Pinnacle Trail, but dogs should not be allowed into the lake to swim after wildlife.

At 1.2 miles the rocks are gone, but the real climbing begins. Wood steps are built into the hillside at some points, with occasional benches for taking a breather. The trail is steep, sandy, and slippery in spots. Be sure to check your dog's progress and give her water and rest stops. The trail demands relentless climbing until the summit.

A large boulder to climb awaits you at the summit. If you have a terrier or pug-size dog, it will be easy to lift him up as you climb the rock. Larger dogs will have problems here, and since it is better not to stress them out, turn around here or take them on a different hike in the park.

If you do have a small dog you can lift up to the top, this is a great place to relax. There are plenty of large boulders where you can catch your breath, have a snack, and drink in the view. Kings Pinnacle is 1705 feet. From this vantage, you can see as far as Charlotte to the east and US 74 and Kings Mountain to the west. Scrub oak and Virginia pine frame the views, and you are very likely to see hawks and vultures swooping on the air currents. Hold on tight to the dogs on this perch, however. There are steep, high drop-offs and no guardrails.

After a sufficient rest, head carefully back down the Pinnacle Trail—the steep, well-worn slope can be treacherously slippery. About 1 mile from the summit, come to the Turnback Trail on the right. For different views of the forest and a brief section along a small stream, take this route back to the trailhead.

36. Crowders Lake Trail—Crowders Mountain State Park

Loop: 1 mile
Hiking time: 20 minutes
Best time to hike: Year-round
High point: 850 feet
Elevation gain: 30 feet
Difficulty: Easy
Rules and fees: Dogs must be on a 6-foot leash and attended at all times
Maps: USGS Kings Mountain; Crowders Mountain State Park
Contact: Crowders Mountain State Park, 704-853-5375; *www .ncparks.gov*

Getting there: Heading south, take Interstate 85 to exit 13 to Edgewood Road. At the top of the ramp turn left onto Edgewood Road. At the first stoplight, turn right onto Franklin Boulevard/US 74 and drive about 2 miles. At the second stoplight, turn left onto Sparrow Springs Road. Continue on Sparrow Springs Road for about 2 miles, and turn right to continue on Sparrow Springs Road. In less than 1 mile, turn right into the park entrance. Drive past the turnoff for the park office and turn into the first parking lot on the left for the Crowders Lake Trail.

Most of the trails in Crowders Mountain State Park are steep, rugged, rough workouts for human and canine hikers. For those looking for a less strenuous way to enjoy nature and get away from the city—the park sits just to the west of Gastonia and Charlotte—the park offers picnic areas, a campground, canoe rentals, and fishing. For the dogs' enjoyment, two hiking trails are shorter, more laid-back, and easier on the paws. Both the Fern Trail, a 0.8-mile nature walk through the woods, and the 1-mile Crowders Lake Trail are appropriate for almost any breeds, as long as they are on a leash. Dogs might find the lake trail a little more interesting for one reason—ducks. The trail completely circles the 9-acre, human-made lake on a soft, level trail with a barely measurable elevation gain.

Once in the parking area, go down the path toward the lake. Since it is a loop trail, you can go either way—a counterclockwise route is described here. Turn right and follow a blaze of a hiker on a blue circle background, although it would be nearly impossible to get lost on this trail. A few hundred feet into the trail, cross a bridge and walk along a trail lined in a variety of oaks, as well as cedar, pine, dogwood, red maple, sourwood, and many more hardwoods.

This is a good springtime trail since the park is home to more than 200 species of trees, shrubs, and wildflowers. Along with flowering dogwood and mountain laurel trees, a multitude of wildflowers bloom in spring, including purple violet, trillium, ox-eye daisies, and jack-in-the-pulpit, and all offer tempting colors and scents to entice a dog's nose and eyes.

Autumn is also a nice hiking season here with fall wildflowers such as aster and goldenrod in bloom, along with the colorful change of leaves. Winter can also be rewarding when leaves have dropped and opened up more views.

At 0.2 mile, come to steps on the right that lead up to a picnic area. Head up here for lunch or continue on the easy trail that hugs the lake, with occasional benches and plenty of viewpoints and places to get close to the water to watch canoes and ducks floating by.

Although dogs will most likely want to splash, they should not be allowed to submerge or swim after the ducks, and they should always be leashed. The lake contains leeches, and swimming is prohibited. As always, bring extra drinking water for your four-legged hiking buddies.

Carol stops to chat with her Llasahpoo, Pup Pup, on the Crowders Mountain Lake Trail.

At 0.3 mile, come to a bridge over a slow-running stream. Start to round the lake, heading southeast, with the towering peak of Crowders Mountain (Hike 37) in the distance—with a summit of 1625 feet, it is the shorter of the two peaks in the park. The other is Kings Pinnacle at 1705 feet (Hike 35).

Continue through a stretch of pine trees, with lots of running ground cedar at the trail's edges. At 0.7 mile, the trail splits. Follow the blazes to the left, walking close to the lake. Soon you will be out of the woods with an open view of the lake. Pass by the canoe rentals and the fishing pier. At 0.9 mile, turn right, back to the parking lot.

37. Tower and Backside Trails—Crowders Mountain State Park

Loop: 3 miles
Hiking time: 2 hours
Best time to hike: Year-round
High point: 1625 feet
Elevation gain: 725 feet
Difficulty: Strenuous
Rules and fees: Dogs must be on a 6-foot leash
Maps: USGS Kings Mountain; Crowders Mountain State Park
Contact: Crowders Mountain State Park, 704-853-5375; *www .ncparks.gov*

Getting there: Heading south, take Interstate 85 to exit 13 to Edgewood Road. At the top of the ramp turn left onto Edgewood Road. At the first stoplight, turn right onto Franklin Boulevard/US 74 and drive about 2 miles. At the second stoplight, turn left onto Sparrow Springs Road. Continue on Sparrow Springs Road for about 2 miles, and turn left on Linwood Road, turning right into the park at the Linwood Road Access.

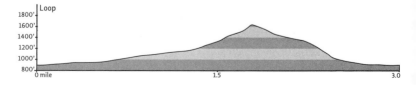

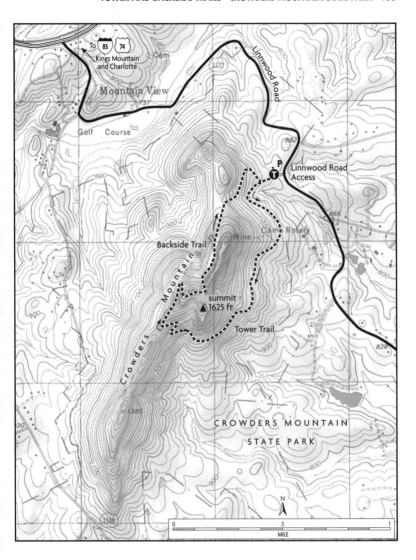

The 1625-foot-high summit of Crowders Mountain is the shorter of the two monadnocks towering over Crowders Mountain State Park. Its summit, topped with a TV and radio tower, can be seen from many miles away.

The park is the largest nearby natural area for hiking, making it extremely popular with the local residents of Kings Mountain, Gastonia, and Charlotte, which sits about 20 miles to the east. Many people visit the park with their dogs. Although the parking lots on most weekends of the year are completely full, the park is not named for its crowds, but for Ulrich Crowder, who owned the land in the late 1700s. In the 1960s, when the land was proposed for mining, local residents banded together to preserve the area, and the state park was established in 1974. Crowders Mountain, with its sheer cliffs ranging up to 150 feet in height, is a registered natural heritage area.

Although Kings Pinnacle, at 1705 feet, is the higher of the two peaks (see Hike 35), the Crowders Mountain summit is a more popular destination, with four different access trails. Two—the Tower Trail and the Backside Trail—are described here, combined to form a 3-mile loop that is easier for most dogs to navigate than the more strenuous Pinnacle Trail.

Start the Tower Trail at the Linwood Access parking area by walking past the restrooms on a wide gravel road, which is closed except for service vehicles. At 0.2 mile, the Backside Trail, blazed in orange hexagons, turns to the right, into the woods. This summit trail is shorter, but steeper, and is easier to hike on the return loop. Instead, keep walking straight on the Tower Trail, following a blue square blaze. The trail is lined in tall pine and oak trees and is very pretty in fall.

After walking 1 mile you have gained about 200 feet in elevation. In late fall and winter when the leaves are down, views sweep to the southeast and the communications tower on the summit is visible ahead and to the right.

At 1.3 miles, the climbing is steady and arduous. Even though this is a wide road with easy footing, and no rocks or obstacles, the relentless climbing makes it a tough hike, and it is only for dogs in good condition. There are no water sources, so bring plenty for the pooches to drink.

At 1.5 miles the Rock Top Trail, blazed in red circles, crosses over the road and into the woods. Continue on the gravel road, and with one last, steep push, arrive at 2 miles at the summit. The first view is not pretty as you are faced with the ugly metal radio tower, but there is an upside—hawks and raptors swooping off their perches on the tower rungs, gliding on air currents overhead, and causing a loud creak when they light again on the tower.

Walk past the tower and metal fencing, following the red circle Rock Top blazes over the rocks to arrive at massive rock outcroppings that lead to more sweeping views. These perches are picturesque, but they can be hazardous. Park regulations require dogs to be on six-foot leashes, and

Tullah, a Harlequin Great Dane-Dalmatian, walks on the Tower Trail in Crowders Mountain State Park.

this is definitely the place to make sure they are secure. On a clear day, you can see the city skyline of Charlotte, 26 miles away.

To make a return loop, continue past the rocks to the orange-blazed Backside Trail, and start descending extremely steep wood stairs—334 in all. These can be slippery in fall if they are covered in dry leaves. At the bottom of the steps, look back up at the cliff faces, where rock climbers are often scaling their way to the top.

Keep descending a wide, wooded trail with easy footing, and at 2.4 miles, come to a bench by the fork with the Crowders Mountain Trail to the left. Continue straight, and at 2.8 miles turn left onto the Tower Trail, which leads back to the parking lot.

38. Fern Nature Trail—New River State Park

Loop: 1.2 miles
Hiking time: 45 minutes
Best time to hike: Year-round
High point: 2760 feet
Elevation gain: 140 feet
Difficulty: Easy
Rules and fees: Dogs must be on a leash no longer than 6 feet
Maps: USGS Jefferson; New River State Park
Contact: New River State Park, 336-982-2587; *www.ncparks.gov*

Getting there: From western North Carolina, take Interstate 40 east to the Blue Ridge Parkway north to US 221. Continue north on US 221, driving through Jefferson. Turn right on NC 88 east. Cross the New River and turn left on Wagoner Road (SR 1590), which leads to the park office and the parking area for the Fern Nature Trail.

The park has two other access areas—the US 221 access and the Alleghany County access, which also have hiking trails. A new 13,000-square foot visitor center with auditorium and exhibit hall opened at the US 221 access in June 2007.

New River State Park sits in a fertile, low-lying valley and is well-known for its canoe trails down the winding river, but the lush woods that hug the riverbanks offer great, shady trails for dogs and their people to hike. A short, 1.2-mile round-trip loop on the Fern Nature Trail gets you up close with the river. If combined with another short, scenic hike at nearby Mount Jefferson State Park (about 8 miles to the west), it is a great way to explore this northwestern part of the state with your dog.

From the parking area, walk away from the canoe ramp toward the open field. Walk through the field, past the Butterfly Garden, and continue 0.2 mile on a gravel road, passing by the picnic area and campground, to reach the trailhead for the Fern Nature Trail on the right. The trailhead has a box with booklets that correspond to numbered posts with which you can guide yourself through a natural history lesson along the trail.

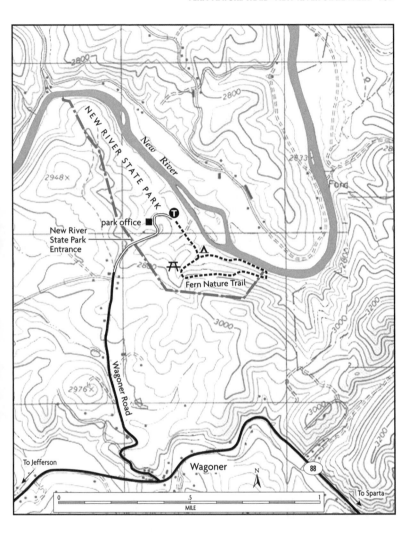

Enter a cool, deep, dense forest with a small creek trickling by on the right, which no doubt will lure dogs instantly for a drink. The soil is rich and soft for paw pads, and the heavy canopy offers plenty of shade.

At 0.3 mile arrive at a fork intersecting with the Running Cedar Trail, which veers to the right. (By combining the Fern Nature Trail and the Running Cedar Trail you could complete a 2-mile loop). Continue straight ahead for the Fern Nature Trail loop, following orange blazes. At 0.5 mile, turn and head down imbedded wooden stairs, passing by sign number 5 and through an area of rhododendron known as a slick or hells, since

The New River is thought to be one of the oldest rivers in North America.

it is so dense that humans could not navigate it without a machete, and where animals seek shelter from predators.

At 0.6 mile you can start to see the New River—thought to be the old-est river in America and one of the oldest in the world—peeking out to the left through the oaks, maples, hickories, and pines. The trail edges offer a lot to tempt your four-legged companions—colorful wildflowers, fluffy ferns, woodland creatures such as snakes and skunks—but an abundance of poison ivy lies in wait in the underbrush. Be aware that animals, without contracting a rash themselves, can carry the ivy's poison on their paws and coats and pass it on to people.

At 0.8 mile, curve to the left toward the river and start to descend. In summer the foliage is very dense and it is hard to see through the trees, but you do get glimpses of the river, where you will often see people wading out to fish and canoes sliding by. You can get close enough to the river in a couple of places for dogs to take a dip—an especially welcome treat for them in summer.

Turn left, away from the river, at 1.1 miles and head uphill. Take a right onto a gravel road and head back through the picnic area and field to the parking area.

39. Summit and Rhododendron Trails—Mount Jefferson State Natural Area

Loop: 1.4 miles
Hiking time: 1 hour
Best time to hike: Year-round
High point: 4683 feet
Elevation gain: 203 feet
Difficulty: Moderate
Rules and fees: Dogs must be on a leash no longer than 6 feet
Maps: USGS Jefferson; Mount Jefferson State Natural Area
Contact: Mount Jefferson State Natural Area, 336-246-9653; *www .ncparks.gov*

Getting there: From Boone, take US 221 north. After crossing the intersection with NC 163, follow the signs to the park by turning right on

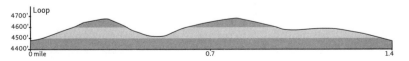

SR 1152. From here it is 1 mile to the park entrance. Continue past the park office to the picnic area parking lot to start the Summit Trail.

Mount Jefferson State Natural Area, named for Thomas Jefferson, whose family owned land nearby, is a 600-acre state natural area in Ashe County that is botanically diverse, scenically lovely, and perfect for hiking with dogs. Established as a state park in 1956, it was renamed as a state natural area in 1975 because of its significant population of rare plants. If you approach the park from the southwest, an overlook on the Blue Ridge Parkway (at milepost 266.8) allows you to admire Mount Jefferson from a distance before you get there.

A nice time to visit is in early June when wildflowers are abundant and the Catawba rhododendron are in bloom, but this is an enjoyable trail any time of year, including in fall—when the many hardwood leaves morph into beautiful colors.

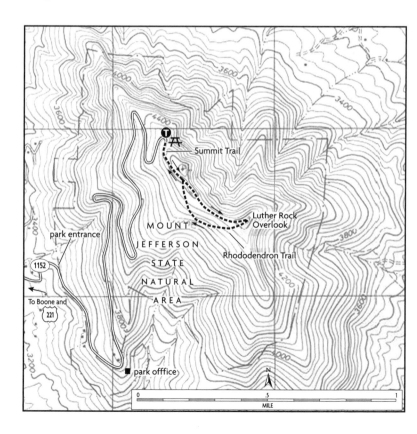

Glenn and Shelby enjoy the views from Luther Rock on the Rhododendron Trail.

The Summit Trail, which can be combined with the Rhododendron Trail to form a loop, starts at an elevation of about 4480 feet at the picnic area. Park maps are available at the trailhead.

Walk through the picnic area, and after a couple hundred feet the trail passes by the restrooms, then branches with the Rhododendron Trail to the right. This is where the loop trail will emerge on the return, but for now continue straight on the path ahead for the summit. At 0.2 mile, come to a signboard describing different natural features that change with the seasons. Turn left here, climbing a steep gravel road to the summit, which you reach at 0.3 mile.

The scene here is not spectacular—a fire tower hovers over a sign that says "Danger—Cliff, Steep Slopes." Pass under the tower to see the view from the summit, but there's a precipitous drop-off, so make sure dogs are well restrained. Fields, farmland, and the town of Jefferson spread out with some peaks in the distance, but the view is not remarkable. A lookout farther along the Rhododendron Trail is much better. Retrace your steps to the signboard, and bear left to continue on the Rhododendron Trail, a self-guiding trail with interpretive signposts.

Follow the orange-red circular blazes and read the various signs about the park's geology and natural history as you go. Pass through a diverse and lush forest of maple, rhododendron, mountain laurel, azalea, chestnut oak, black locust, ash, and birch. Many wildflowers in spring dot the trail edges, including fire pinks, daisies, and violets.

Walking along a steep cliff on the left, come to the "Mountain Rocks" sign, which describes the park's dominant rock—amphibolite, a metamorphic stone composed of dark minerals that include hornblende and feldspar. At 0.6 mile come to an overlook on the left, and then another signboard with rotating features on topics such as mountain balds or trees native to the region. Turn left here for Luther Rock Overlook, a large outcropping at 4680 feet elevation with great views, including the New River. (New River State Park, about 8 miles to the east, is another great place to take the dogs for a hike.) While up on these rocks, be sure to hold on tight to dogs.

Backtrack to the interpretive sign describing the area's heath balds, which are unique natural communities in forest clearings dominated by shrubby vegetation at elevations above 4000 feet, like Luther Rock. Continue on trail past the sign and start to descend rapidly. Pass by more signs, and at about 1.3 miles emerge from the woods at a fork. Turn left and backtrack to the picnic and parking area.

40. Stone Mountain Summit Trail—Stone Mountain State Park

Round-trip: 3.6 miles
Hiking time: 2 hours
Best time to hike: Year-round
High point: 2305 feet
Elevation gain: 570 feet
Difficulty: Strenuous
Rules and fees: Dogs must be on a leash no longer than 6 feet
Maps: USGS Glade Valley; Stone Mountain State Park
Contact: Stone Mountain State Park, 336-957-8185; *www .ncparks.gov*

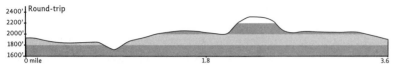

Getting there: From Elkin, take Interstate 77 north to US 21 west. Drive for 10 miles and veer left onto Traphill Road. Go 5 miles and turn right on John P. Frank Parkway. Follow the parkway into Stone Mountain State Park and around to the picnic area. Park there.

The star of this show is the big, bald face for which the park is named—Stone Mountain. The 600-foot granite dome is so conspicuously colossal, you just feel compelled to stare at it, want to photograph it, and, of course, feel drawn to hike up to its summit. In addition to the immense beauty of Stone Mountain, the 14,400-acre park has trout streams and hiking trails, a campground and picnic area, and a long cultural history on display at the Hutchinson Homestead. Sitting right under the massive dome, the homestead has a self-guiding trail that passes by a historic log cabin, barn, blacksmith shop, and other remnants of a nineteenth-century farm.

The park's signature trail, the Stone Mountain Loop Trail, which makes a 4.5-mile loop around the summit, passing by many of the park's interesting features, starts with an extremely strenuous climb that is just not fun with dogs. An easier way to enjoy a hike, the summit views, and some waterfalls is to take an out-and-back trail, starting in the picnic area across from the visitor center.

Follow blue blazes through the picnic area, past the restrooms, on a paved path lined in red maples, white pines, and chestnut oaks. About 0.1 mile up the path, turn left at the sign that points to "Stone Mountain Trail" in 0.5 mile. At 0.25 mile, enter a rhododendron and mountain laurel forest, then come to a bridge across a creek. The trail enters a wide open field and soon returns to the woods.

At 0.5 mile into the trail, a surprise appears—the remnants of an old stone chimney—and a fork in the trail. If you wish to see some pretty falls before heading for the summit, turn left here for a 0.2-mile walk to Stone Mountain Falls and follow the red blazes. Arrive at the first trickles of the falls sweeping down a rock face on the left, protected by a fence to prevent people from sliding down with the water (be sure to hold on

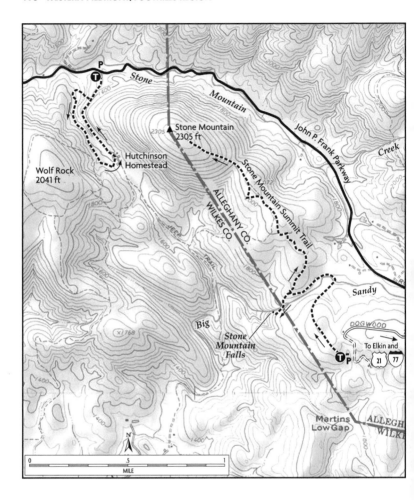

to dogs here), and then come to steep wood stairs. These lead down to a platform for a view at the bottom of the waterfall. Backtrack from here to the fork by the chimney and bear to the left for the summit.

At 1.4 miles, come to the first grand vista stretching out in front of a large rock outcropping. Continue on another 0.2 mile to an expanse of exposed granite with a perfect view of Stone Mountain off to the right, often accentuated with the sight of soaring hawks. The rock outcropping here is wide and flat and perfect for a lunch and daydreaming break, but watch dogs carefully—the drops are a long way down. This is a trail perfectly suited for fall hiking, when the cooler weather makes the steep climbing more comfortable and the changing leaves make the views vibrant with color.

Continue walking northwest, back into the woods for a bit before arriving at another steep, massive rock face, and heading straight up on the last push toward the summit. Arrive on top of Stone Mountain in 2 miles, at 2305 feet elevation. Surprisingly, the big rock is not bald on top—it has a healthy head covering of pines, hemlocks, and oaks that perfectly frame the view of the surrounding mountains. Enjoy the scene before backtracking, making your way carefully on the slick, steep rock faces to the picnic area.

For a different view of Stone Mountain and a 1-mile moderate, round-trip hike, drive 2 miles through the park to the Hutchinson Homestead parking area. Take the trail there through the woods or walk on the road

The face of Stone Mountain looms over the Hutchinson Homestead at Stone Mountain State Park.

to the homestead site, which sits just below the towering rock. On cool, clear days, you can often see tiny specks on the rock—climbers making their way up the many routes.

41. Jomeokee and Sassafras Trails—Pilot Mountain State Park

Loop: 1.5 miles
Hiking time: 80 minutes
Best time to hike: Year-round
High point: 2300 feet
Elevation gain: 280 feet
Difficulty: Moderate
Rules and fees: Dogs must be on a leash no longer than 6 feet
Maps: USGS Pinnacle; Pilot Mountain State Park
Contact: Pilot Mountain State Park, 336-325-2355; *www .ncparks.gov*

Getting there: From Winston-Salem, take US 52 northwest for 22 miles to the Pilot Mountain State Park exit. Turn left, then left again into the mountain section of the park, where the park office is located. Follow the main park road past the office to the Summit Area parking area for the Jomeokee Trail.

Just a half-hour drive north of the city of Winston-Salem is a natural wonder jutting up from the earth. Pilot Mountain State Park's namesake—the 200-foot-high monadnock (an isolated rock mountain)—is something impressive to see. While you cannot climb to its summit, the giant rock can be viewed from many vantages, including the two short loop trails described here. The Jomeokee Trail lets you completely circle the rock's base and gaze up its massive cliff faces, while the Sassafras Trail lets you see the whole rock from a distance.

A hike on the Jomeokee Trail brings you close up to the towering cliff face of the Big Pinnacle.

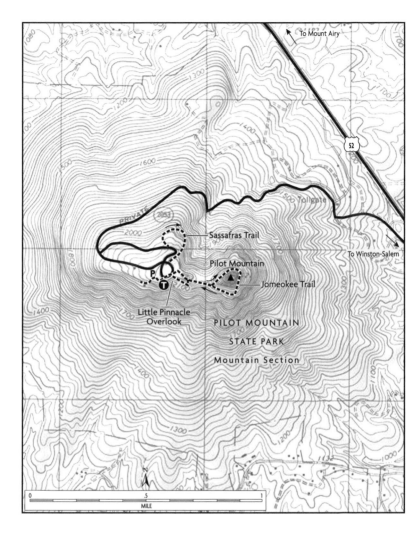

The park, which comprises 3700 acres of woods, trails, rock outcrops, and rivers, includes the northern mountain section, plus two river sections surrounding the Yadkin River. It was established in 1968, to protect the natural resources found at the mountain (and to prevent overuse from eager tourists and rock climbers) and to offer a place of recreation in the Piedmont. Pilot Mountain is actually two peaks—Little Pinnacle and Big Pinnacle—connected by a saddle. Big Pinnacle is the well-known monadnock. Once allowed, climbing the Big Pinnacle is now prohibited, and the peak must be loved from afar.

One way to get up close is by hiking the Jomeokee Trail, named for the Saura Indian word meaning "great guide" or "pilot." A lone remnant of the ancient Sauratown Mountains, the 2421-foot summit resisted erosion through the millennia and now is a conspicuous beacon in the relatively flat Piedmont.

From the Summit Area parking lot, start walking past the restrooms toward the Little Pinnacle Overlook. You are actually walking on the ridgeline of the park's lower summit, which offers great views of Big Pinnacle, resembling a majestic cupcake with evergreen frosting.

Brandy, a long-haired Chihuahua, prefers to be carried along the Sassafras Trail by Chrystelle and Brandon.

The best time to hike with dogs is in fall when the air is cooler and the beautiful fall colors accent the mountains. Most of the park's vegetation resembles a higher, alpine environment with evergreen rhododendron, mountain laurel, white pine, and pitch pine, but it also includes an assortment of oaks, maples, and other hardwoods.

After taking in the view from the Little Pinnacle Overlook, backtrack to the intersection and turn right for the Jomeokee Trail. Descend stone steps among mountain laurel, maples, and rhododendron, with Pilot Mountain looming ahead. Come to a stone bench and sign that says, "Warning! Stay on marked trail." People and dogs should heed the warning. Drop-offs are steep.

At 0.35 mile, pass the turnoff for the Ledge Spring Trail on the right, continuing straight. Ascend stone steps, come to a fork, and turn left. Massive rock looms overhead as you are walking beside the monolith. The environment has an otherworldly "Land of the Lost" feel.

Continue walking up and down stone steps as you circle the rock, which is on your right, close enough to touch, and a sweeping valley view peeking through the trees to the left. The footing is rough and rocky, so it is best suited for dogs used to this type of terrain. At about 0.8 mile, you will have circled back to the trail intersection. Turn left, and once back at the trailhead, turn right to start the 0.5-mile-long Sassafras Trail.

A sign at the trailhead warns hikers to stay on the trail and keep away from the wooden fence, which was built to protect visitors from losing their footing on the steep cliffs. Start descending set-in wood steps among pitch pines, a variety of oaks, and, of course, sassafras trees. Beyond the fence on the right is a nice view of Big Pinnacle through the trees. This earth-and-gravel trail is well used and is subject to erosion, another reason to stay on trail and not create shortcuts, even though dogs might often be tempted to wander, especially to sniff the pungent galax plants.

Pass through groves of mountain laurel and rhododendron, scarlet oak and pine, and at 0.15 mile from the Sassafras trailhead, come to a fork. Go left to walk the loop in a clockwise direction. Soon arrive at a bench, and continue descending. At 0.3 mile from the Sassafras trailhead, pass a view of the valley and then start to climb. As you round the loop and head back to the trailhead, there are plenty of views of Big Pinnacle through the trees. Arrive back at the fork, turn left, and ascend the steps to finish the loop, and at the trailhead, turn right for the parking area.

42. Densons Creek Nature Trail— Uwharrie National Forest

Loop: 2.2 miles
Hiking time: 1.5 hours
Best time to hike: Year-round
High point: 535 feet
Elevation loss: 135 feet
Difficulty: Easy
Rules and fees: Dogs must be on a leash no longer than 6 feet
Maps: USGS Biscoe; Uwharrie National Forest
Contact: Uwharrie National Forest, 910-576-6391; *www.cs.unca.edu/nfsnc*

Getting there: The trailhead is behind the Uwharrie National Forest district office. From Troy, drive east on NC 24/27 for 2 miles. Look for the brown Forest Service sign for the office on the left. Park around behind the office, which is open 8:00 AM to 4:30 PM Monday through Friday, and start at the trailhead sign.

The Densons Creek Nature Trail is one of the shorter, easier trails in the Uwharrie National Forest, which sits in the central Piedmont region of North Carolina about an hour east of Charlotte. This 53,000-acre forest is the smallest of the state's four national forests, but its lakes, rivers, and shaded trails offer a great recreational outlet close to the more urban areas of North Carolina.

The Uwharrie National Forest was created in 1961 in Montgomery, Randolph, and Davidson counties, making it one of the newest in the national forest system. It is named for the Uwharrie Mountains, some of the oldest in North America.

The Densons Creek Nature Trail is an interpretive route made up of a 0.75-mile loop within a larger, 2.2-mile loop. A brochure available at the Forest Service office guides hikers along numbered stops. The trail offers a great, wooded way to stretch your dog's legs if you are traveling across the state, as well as an education in nature studies for the people on the trip.

Start the trail directly behind the office (open weekdays only) and follow the path blazed with white rectangles. Enter a grove of mountain laurel, rhododendron, tulip poplar, dogwood, maple, oak, and a lot of other hardwoods.

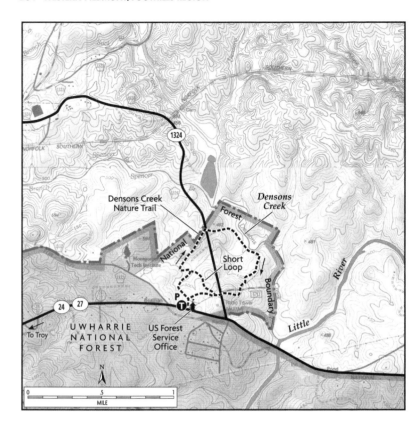

At the first intersection, bear left to follow the trail in a clockwise direction. At 0.3 mile, round a bend by a large, tall white pine and holly trees. The trail is well trampled, so it is easy to follow even though the blazes are very faded and hard to spot. In spring, the mountain laurel blooms with pink and white blossoms. In summer, the trail is well shaded with hardwood leaves, which also offer a colorful buffet in autumn.

At 0.4 mile, come to a bridge and a bench, one of many along the trail for stopping to study the trail key, identify the surrounding trees, or quietly look for wildlife. Some of the animals that inhabit this area include rabbits, squirrels, wild turkeys, and deer. The largest predator inhabiting the woods is the bobcat—keeping your dog on a leash will help to prevent unwanted encounters with these cats. Hunting is permitted in the forest, so be aware of hunting seasons—usually from October through April—and protect yourself and your dog by wearing something blaze orange.

Just after the bridge, a fork in the trail and a signpost signal the shorter loop to the right leading back to the parking area. To get more of a hike, continue straight, crossing a bridge to follow the longer Densons Creek Loop Trail. To the left is a turnoff for the Fitness Trail. Stay straight, winding through pines and hardwoods.

Arlene and Shelby take a stroll along the Densons Creek Nature Trail in the Uwharrie National Forest.

At just under a mile, come to SR 1324. Be sure to have dogs leashed here when crossing the road and picking up the white blaze on the other side. Come to a sign for the ranger station, turn right here, and start a slight uphill climb.

In another 0.2 mile, cross another road, bear right, then left, following the trail blazes. Dogs will probably bury their noses on the trail edges, picking up the skunklike scent from the abundant galax, as well as the Christmas fern and running cedar plants.

After another mile, you will arrive back at SR 1324. Cross the road and come to a sign indicating that the ranger station is 0.25 mile away. Continue on a relatively flat path for the remainder of the hike, occasionally stepping over chunks of quartz poking out of the ground. Arrive back at the Forest Service office in just about an hour and a half.

Running cedar, also called ground pine, grows profusely along parts of the Densons Creek Nature Trail.

EASTERN PIEDMONT/ COASTAL REGION

43. Occoneechee Mountain Trail —Occoneechee Mountain State Natural Area

Loop: 2 miles
Hiking time: 1 hour
Best time to hike: Year-round
High point: 867 feet
Elevation gain: 250 feet
Difficulty: Moderate
Rules and fees: Dogs must be on a leash no longer than 6 feet
Maps: USGS Hillsborough; Occoneechee Mountain State Natural Area
Contact: Occoneechee Mountain State Natural Area/Eno River State Park office, 919-383-1686; *www.ncparks.gov*

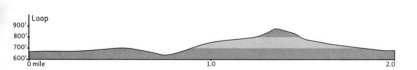

Getting there: Traveling on Interstate 85 near Durham, take exit 164. Turn north on Churton Street, then turn left at the stoplight onto Mayo Street. At the next stop sign, turn left onto Orange Grove Road. Turn right onto Virginia Cates Road, and follow the signs to the gravel parking area, where there are pit toilets and picnic tables.

Occoneechee Mountain State Natural Area, at only 190 acres, is one of the smallest units in the North Carolina State Parks system. Its rewards, however, are immeasurable for the natural beauty offered amid one of the state's biggest urban areas—the Triangle region of Raleigh, Durham, and Chapel Hill.

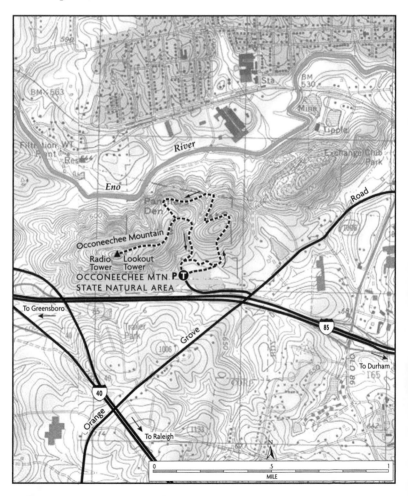

Alexandra and her Sheltie, Kimi, take a rest stop on the Occoneechee Mountain Trail.

Start the trail by continuing down the gravel driveway that led into the park, away from the entrance, and in about 100 yards come to a fork. Turn right at the signboard, passing by a residence on the left, to walk the Occoneechee Mountain Trail in a counterclockwise loop. Walk through a mowed grass area lined with shrubs and then across a field lined in young pine trees.

At 0.1 mile, fishing ponds are off to the right and a field with white arrowhead trail markers is straight ahead. Follow the white arrows and then the red blazes into a forest of tall maples, tulip poplars, skinny pines, and sourwoods. At 0.3 mile, start climbing. The forest floor is soft on little paws and offers an abundance of wildflowers and pungent galax for wet noses to sniff during spring and fall.

In another 0.1 mile, you will come to the turnoff for the Brown Elfin Knob Trail to the left. This is a 0.2-mile connector that shortens up the loop to the other side of the Occoneechee Mountain Trail. This tiny trail is named for the brown elfin butterfly, a rare species except for a large population that lives within this park. Instead of taking this little trail, keep walking straight on the Occoneechee Mountain Trail and soon start to descend. The ground gets a little rocky here as you come into a mountain laurel and rhododendron grove and the occasional bench for sitting a while.

At about 0.7 mile, arrive at an opening in the woods cut for powerlines and turn left, walking down a rocky, dirt road. Bear left, back into the forest, and start up a series of wooden stairs. The trail continues to climb and wind through forest among large chestnut oaks, maples, rhododendrons, and mountain laurels. Soon come to a fence that leads to an overlook on the right. At the time of this writing, a sign warned hikers not to approach the overlook because of unstable ground. Park staff were in the process of repairing damage from a 2002 rock slide. The area overlooking an old rock quarry was scheduled to reopen in spring 2007.

Continue following the red blazes and soon come to a fork at a gravel road. If the dogs are up for a little more of a hike, turn right for the summit in 0.3 mile. The 867-foot summit is the highest point in Orange County, but there is no view, just a radio tower, so people looking for a vista might want to skip it.

Backtrack from here 0.3 mile to the fork, keep going straight, passing the other end of the Brown Elfin Knob Trail on the left, and at 2 miles arrive back at the parking area.

44. Buckquarter Creek Trail— Eno River State Park

Loop: 1.5 miles
Hiking time: 1 hour
Best time to hike: Year-round
High point: 535 feet
Elevation gain: 110 feet
Difficulty: Easy
Rules and fees: Dogs must be on a leash no longer than 6 feet
Maps: USGS Durham NW; Eno River State Park Western Trails
Contact: Eno River State Park office, 919-383-1686; *www .ncparks.gov*

Getting there: *From the Durham area,* take Interstate 85 to exit 173 to Cole Mill Road. Stay on Cole Mill Road for 5 miles to the Fews Ford Access. *From Hillsborough,* take Interstate 85 north to exit 170 onto US 70 west. Turn right onto Pleasant Green Road and left onto Cole Mill Road, which ends at the park. Follow signs past the park office to the first parking lot on the right and look for the Buckquarter Creek trailhead sign.

Fall is a great time of year to hike with dogs in Eno River State Park. The leaves of hardwood trees are turning Thanksgiving colors, and while surrounding game lands allow hunting, it is prohibited in this state park, so you can hike the woods worry free with your dogs, although they must be on a leash at all times.

The park, a 3900-acre natural area northwest of Durham, surrounds 14 miles of the 33-mile Eno River as it flows through woods and wilderness and past historic home and mill sites, eventually running with the Little

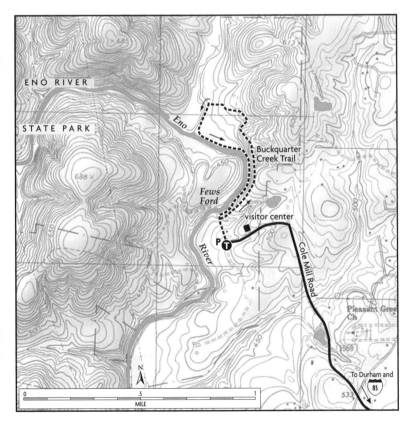

The Piper-Cox Museum sits at the trailhead for the Buckquarter Creek Trail in Eno River State Park.

and Flat Rivers to form the Neuse. The park offers camping, picnicking, canoeing, fishing, and 24 miles of hiking trails. Start the Buckquarter Creek Trail at the Piper-Cox Museum parking lot, entering a forest of maples behind the trailhead sign and descending on steps to the Eno River. Pass by Fews Ford—a wide river crossing—and turn to the right, heading upstream and following the trail signs. Come to a fork and turn right, but avoid taking the nearly immediate right path, which leads up steps to the park office—and keep going straight, following a red blotchy blaze. Climb among mountain laurel, maple, and oak while listening to the river bubbling along to the left.

At 0.2 mile, descend a set of wood stairs, come to a dip in the path, then start ascending wood steps passing through tall river birches and oaks. The path widens, and you are walking on soft earth floor with some scattered rocks. It is a very tranquil trail, except for the occasional sound of deer breaking branches as they run through the woods.

At 0.45 mile, arrive at a short boardwalk and the intersection with the Ridge Trail, which leads off to the right and connects with the Knight Trail.

Stay to the left to stay on the Buckquarter Creek Trail. Keep crossing little boardwalks that cover muddy patches to help prevent trail erosion.

At 0.7 mile, continue walking straight when you come to a bridge that crosses the creek to the right, leading to the Holden Mill Trail. At about 1 mile, the trail starts to hug the edge of the Eno River, giving easy access for dogs to dip their paws, although they must remain on a leash even in the water. Large, flat rocks allow you to rock hop and provide seats for picnicking or sightseeing from mid-river. Opportunities for wildlife viewing are numerous here if you can sit still and quiet and keep the dogs from splashing or barking. Beavers are elusive, but their presence is marked everywhere on gnawed logs. They are more likely to be spotted in the early mornings or at dusk. Other park inhabitants include owls, wood ducks, great blue herons, and belted kingfishers.

As you continue downstream, walking becomes a little tricky with rugged rocks and large roots right along the bank. At 1.2 miles is a lovely little cascade, which can be viewed more easily by climbing the staircase here. After descending the other side of the stairs you will come to an interpretive sign detailing the needs of a healthy river. Continue the path to Fews Ford, where you turn left, then right, going back up steps to the parking area.

45. Sals Branch Trail—William B. Umstead State Park

Loop: 2.75 miles
Hiking time: 1.5 hours
Best time to hike: Year-round
High point: 450 feet
Elevation gain: 100 feet
Difficulty: Easy
Rules and fees: Dogs must be on a leash no longer than 6 feet
Maps: USGS Southeast Durham; William B. Umstead State Park
Contact: William B. Umstead State Park office, 919-571-4170; *www .ncparks.gov*

Getting there: There are two entrances to the park, which sits between Raleigh and Durham in Wake County. The Crabtree Creek section, where the Sals Branch Trail is located, is 10 miles northwest of Raleigh off US 70.

This is also the section where the park visitor center and campground are located. From Interstate 40, turn northeast on Interstate 540 and take the US 70 exit. Drive southeast on US 70, and turn right on Umstead Parkway, which leads to the park office and visitor center.

Just minutes from the congestion of North Carolina's capital city, William B. Umstead State Park is a breath of fresh air and a vision of green. A wildernesslike oasis among some of the state's busiest urban areas, the 5579-acre park named for a conservation-minded governor offers a great place for trail running, fishing, picnicking, boating, biking, and, of course, hiking with your dog.

The Sals Branch Trail is the perfect distance and distraction after work, on a weekend, or for a quick getaway any day during the week. Since mountain bikes are not allowed on this trail, it is also a great path for dogs. The many hardwood trees make autumn a cool and colorful time to hike. The low elevation of Raleigh and the moderate climate also allow for hiking throughout winter. Although leaves provide shade in summer, the hot months can be a little muggy and buggy for dogs.

Big Lake sits along the Sals Branch Trail.

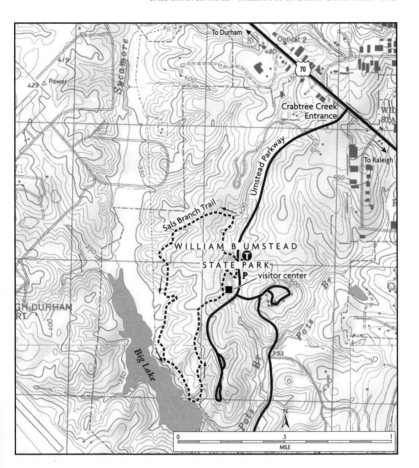

Start the trail behind the visitor center by entering a forest of maple and pine, descending wood stairs down a dirt path, and following a blaze of orange circles. The trail forks immediately. Take the right fork, cross a small bridge over a creek, and then cross another bridge. The water is not deep or fast. Although dogs might want to stop here to wade and splash, it is not suitable for drinking, so be sure to bring along fresh drinking water.

The trail widens out at about 0.1 mile, where the path is lined in beech and birch trees that muffle the still audible traffic from the highway. As you walk along the easy-to-follow trail, sections of dense growth alternate with airy openings in the understory and tall loblolly pines are interspersed with dogwood and sourwood trees. After being heavily logged and cleared in the eighteenth and nineteenth centuries for farmland, the area was purchased and protected in the 1930s. The two separate areas—Crabtree Creek and Reedy Creek—were joined to form one state park in 1966. The forest is still in the process of regrowth.

When you arrive at a sign pointing to the right for the campground, continue straight on the trail. At about 0.75 mile, come to a short boardwalk and bridge, then another bridge, before arriving at a gravel road at the 1-mile point. Cross over the road, entering an almost meadowlike area where the sun sparkles through the many forest openings.

At about 1.4 miles, start ascending a slight uphill and soon come to a powerline opening in the woods. Turn left here on the gravel road to see Big Lake sprawling in front of you. A paved path continues to the southeast end of the lake. To continue on the Sals Branch Trail, turn left at the trail sign and reenter the woods.

At about 2 miles, come back to the gravel road and cross back over. You will soon start to hear the traffic from US 70 again, although the highway is nowhere in sight. Continue following the blazes and cross a couple more footbridges to arrive back at the visitor center parking area.

46. Inspiration Trail—William B. Umstead State Park

Loop: 0.6 mile
Hiking time: 20 minutes
Best time to hike: Year-round
High point: 480 feet
Elevation gain: 100 feet
Difficulty: Easy
Rules and fees: Dogs must be on a leash no longer than 6 feet
Maps: USGS Cary; William B. Umstead State Park
Contact: William B. Umstead State Park office, 919-571-4170; *www .ncparks.gov*

Getting there: There are two entrances to the park, located in Wake County between Raleigh and Durham. The Inspiration Trail is in the Reedy Creek Section, 11 miles west of Raleigh off Interstate 40. Traveling from Raleigh, take I-40 to the Harrison Avenue exit. Continue northeast directly into the park and drive to the picnic area parking lot.

William B. Umstead State Park is named for the U.S. senator who also served as North Carolina governor from 1953 to 1954 and who was dedicated to preserving the state's green spaces. It is a much-needed and well-used natural area close to the urban center of Raleigh.

The park—with two separate entrances quite a distance apart—is almost like two parks in one. It actually used to be a segregated park. The Crabtree Creek Section, which only allowed whites, was opened in 1937, and the Reedy Creek Section, where the Inspiration Trail is located, was set aside for African-Americans in 1950. In 1966 the two sections comprising more than 5500 acres were united as William B. Umstead State Park and opened to everyone.

Trails here meet every canine and human ability, from quick, half-hour trips to multi-hour treks. Two trails start at this loca-tion—the short Inspiration Trail,

Towering loblolly pines are some of the inspirational sights along the Inspiration Trail.

described here, and the much longer Company Mill Trail (Hike 47).

The perfect little after-work pick-me-up, the Inspiration Trail is just what its name implies—a little jolt of outdoor inspiration. It is also a good, quick trail for dogs who are not able to hike far, and it is restricted to foot traffic only, so bicycles and horses are not allowed.

Start the trail by walking into the picnic area and continuing beyond the picnic shelter amid a forest of large tulip poplars. The path starts off rough, uneven, and rocky, so dogs should have tough pads to hike it. Descend steps set into the earth and come to a bridge.

At a fork is a sign for the Inspiration Trail. Go left here, following blue diamond blazes. Go left again and come to the first of many interpretive

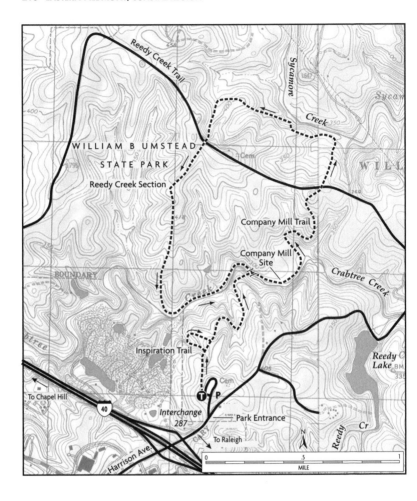

signs—this one describing the eastern red cedar tree—that will grab your attention and make this otherwise very short trail stretch out much longer.

The trees on this trail are definitely the stars of the show. About fifteen signs give the natural and cultural history of the trees common to the Piedmont region. Benches scattered along the trail invite you to sit and glance up at the trees or to quiz yourself on what you have learned.

Some of the featured trees include the loblolly pine, also known as Oldfield or North Carolina pine, the most widely used commercial pine tree in the South. It is also a giant, reaching heights up to 110 feet and 2 to 3 feet in diameter. The tree is distinguished from other pines by its needles, which grow in bundles of three and are 6 to 9 inches long.

Continue walking around the loop in a clockwise direction, learning about trees such as sourwood, white oak, mockernut hickory, American holly, and red maple, which dominate the woods of the park.

At about 0.3 mile, come to a fork and turn right, or south, out of the loop and backtrack to the parking area. If you walk right through the trail without stopping to read the signs, it will only take you 15 minutes, but it is such a pretty, peaceful trail, you will most likely want to linger.

47. Company Mill Trail— William B. Umstead State Park

Loop: 5.8 miles
Hiking time: 3 hours
Best time to hike: Year-round
High point: 525 feet
Elevation gain: 245 feet
Difficulty: Moderate
Rules and fees: Dogs must be on a leash no longer than 6 feet
Maps: USGS Cary; William B. Umstead State Park
Contact: William B. Umstead State Park office, 919-571-4170; *www .ncparks.gov;* Umstead Coalition, *umsteadcoalition.org*

Getting there: There are two entrances to the park, located in Wake County between Raleigh and Durham. The Inspiration Trail is in the Reedy Creek Section, 11 miles west of Raleigh off Interstate 40. Traveling from Raleigh, take I-40 to the Harrison Avenue exit. Continue northeast directly into the park and drive to the picnic area parking lot.

If you have more time to spend exploring William B. Umstead State Park with the dogs than the short, 20-minute trip around the Inspiration Trail (Hike 46), the Company Mill Trail is a good choice. Starting at the same trailhead as the Inspiration Trail, this loop extends nearly 6 miles and

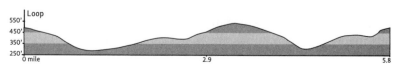

takes at least three leisurely hours to complete as it winds through deep woods and crosses scenic creeks, to every dog's delight. Bicycles and horses are prohibited on the park's hiking trails, making the trails safer for hiking with dogs.

The trail is in the Reedy Creek Section of the park. It is named for a corn and wheat grist mill that was built in 1810 on the banks of Crabtree Creek and became an economic and social center for the local farming community. The mill and dam were damaged by floods in the 1930s. Some stone remnants of the dam can still be seen in the creek.

Start the trail by walking into the picnic area to the right of the rest-rooms and continuing beyond the picnic shelter. Descend steps, and at about 0.1 mile come to a bridge and then a fork where the Inspiration Trail veers to the left. Continue straight, following orange square blazes. Pass by tall loblolly pines, oaks, and maples on a rough trail riddled with rocks and exposed roots.

Head uphill, and at 0.8 mile cross Crabtree Creek on a steel bridge. You can then go either to the left or the right. Turn right to head in a counterclockwise direction, and in 100 feet come to a plaque denoting the Company Mill site. A sandy area here provides easy access to the creek for dogs, who must remain on a leash at all times. Some large, flat rocks midstream and water riffling over smaller rocks create a tranquil setting for lingering.

As you continue, the trail winds along the creek through American holly and red cedar. At 1.5 miles, cross a sturdy wooden bridge with hand railings and continue climbing a steep slope dotted with sparkling quartz rock.

At about 1.85 miles come to the first intersection with the Reedy Creek Trail, one of the 13 miles of multiuse trails in the park, which are made of compacted, fine granite gravel-like screening. Cross over to the woods on the other side. You soon get the feeling of being deep in the woods (only minutes from downtown Raleigh), yet there is a nice, easy, well-marked trail to follow.

At 2.1 miles, come to a fork with a spur leading to the Sycamore Trail (a 7.2-mile trail that heads north into the Crabtree Creek Section of the park). Turn left here to stay on the Company Mill Trail and look for orange blazes.

You will soon be walking along a narrow berm with Sycamore Creek on the right, lots of ferns lining the trail edges, and usually lots of people trail running, hiking with their dogs, and photographing nature scenes, since this area is a crossroads of several trails.

Suka, an Alaskan malamute, takes her owner, Carla, on a walk along the Company Mill Trail in William B. Umstead State Park.

Continue walking through tall pine groves, and at 2.5 miles come to an area with a lot of downed pine logs. At 3 miles cross a creek where dogs might want to take a dip or a drink, and at 3.2 miles arrive once again at an intersection with the Reedy Creek Trail—keep a short leash on dogs here since you are likely to see equestrians or mountain bikers making their way down this route.

Planes and air traffic can soon be heard since the airport is nearby. The trail becomes rocky with lots of quartz chunks scattered on the ground but with enough flat, soft places in between for little paws. Come back to Crabtree Creek running on the right at about 4.1 miles, but the riverbanks are a little too high here to scramble down for a dip. The creek continues to rush along, making for lovely company toward the end of this loop trail.

At about 5 miles arrive back at the big bridge near the Company Mill site, turn right, cross the bridge, then turn left and retrace your steps for 0.8 mile back to the parking area.

48. Falls Lake Trail (Mountains-to-Sea Trail)—Falls Lake State Recreation Area

Round-trip: 5.4 miles
Hiking time: 2 hours
Best time to hike: Late winter, spring, and summer
High point: 340 feet
Elevation gain: 90 feet
Difficulty: Moderate
Rules and fees: Dogs must be on a leash no longer than 6 feet
Map: USGS Creedmoor
Contact: Falls Lake State Recreation Area, 919-676-1027; *www
.ncparks.gov*

Getting there: From Raleigh, take Interstate 440 north to US 1. Follow US 1 north to NC 98 at the town of Wake Forest. Drive about 8 miles to NC 50. Turn right onto NC 50 and travel north 1 mile. The trailhead for the Falls Lake Trail is just north of the turnoff for the park, on the right, before the bridge.

The Falls Lake State Recreation Area encircles 12,000-acre Falls Lake, which lies about 10 miles north of Raleigh. Actually made up of seven individual parks, the Falls Lake area offers boating and fishing, beaches for swimming, campgrounds and picnic areas, and trails for mountain biking and hiking. One of the mini-parks, Sandling Beach State Recreation Area, contains a small hiking loop (Hike 49).

The park was formed in 1981 by the damming of the Neuse River, which created the 22-mile-long lake. Other parcels of woodland, which the state parks department jointly manages with the North Carolina Wildlife Resources Commission, the Army Corps of Engineers, and the North Carolina Division of Forest Resources, total 26,000 acres.

The biggest trail is the 26-mile-long Falls Lake Trail, part of the mighty Mountains-to-Sea Trail, which when finished will stretch 1000 miles from Clingmans Dome in the Great Smoky Mountains in the west to the eastern coast at Jockeys Ridge State Park. The Falls Lake Trail, designated in June 2006 as a National Recreation Trail, is an essential link

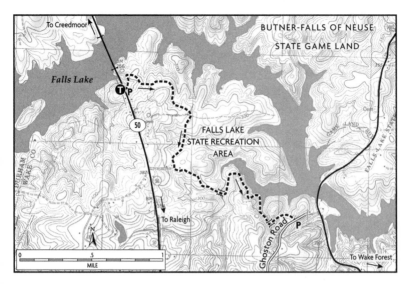

in the Piedmont, since much of the land in the state's midsection is privately owned.

The Falls Lake Trail is divided into ten sections, numbered from east to west, starting at the dam and ending near the park office on NC 50. These sections can be hiked individually as out-and-back trails, using the road crossings as trailheads.

The good news about the Falls Lake Trail is that it is only open to foot traffic, so you will encounter no mountain bikes or horses. However, the trail runs through North Carolina state game land, so hunting is allowed in season, September through May. Park staff strongly recommend wearing blaze orange clothing and putting some on your dogs during hunting season.

The last section, known as Quail Roost, or Section 10, is 2.7 miles one-way. Start at the trailhead sign on NC 50. Enter a shady forest filled with maple, pine, beech, white oak, and holly and follow the white circular blazes that mark the Mountains-to-Sea Trail across the state.

At 0.2 mile, come to the main road that leads into the park. Cross over and look for the white blazes. At 0.4 mile, come to another small road, cross to the other side, and go up a little set of steps. Another 0.2 mile farther, come to a gravel road and cross over, now walking among dogwood, sourwood, and maple, with goldenrod and asters lining the edges in fall.

At 0.7 mile, arrive at the state park boundary with the North Carolina Wildlife Resources Commission game lands. A sign here announces that you are entering a public hunting area where "Hunters may be encountered." Unless you are hiking on Sunday, when hunting is prohibited in the state, it is likely you will run into hunters bearing firearms, as well as hunting dogs that wander off on their own in search of game. Remember to wear blaze orange and put some on your dog.

Turn left here to continue the Falls Lake Trail into an open, sunny area among tall pines. After a few hundred feet, the trail forks again. Turn right here onto an unsigned road. At about 1 mile, turn left back into the woods, following the white dots.

At 1.5 miles, cross a bridge over a creek. As you continue walking, you will start to get glimpses of the lake through the trees on the left. In summer, it is very hard to see through the leaves. The trail narrows, the woods get a little thicker, and you soon arrive at a little path on the left that leads down to a small lake inlet where the dogs can take a dip. Back on the trail, continue to another bridge over a creek, and at 2.7 miles, arrive at Ghoston Road. From here, it is only 23 more miles to the dam, or you can backtrack to where you started.

The Falls Lake Trail hugs Falls Lake for part of its 26 miles.

49. Woodland Nature Trail—Falls Lake State Recreation Area

Loop: 0.75 mile
Hiking time: 40 minutes
Best time to hike: Late March through October
High point: 320 feet
Elevation gain: 50 feet
Difficulty: Easy
Rules and fees: Dogs must be on a leash no longer than 6 feet
Maps: USGS Creedmoor; Falls Lake State Recreation Area
Contact: Falls Lake State Recreation Area, 919-676-1027; *www .ncparks.gov*

Getting there: From Raleigh, take Interstate 440 north to US 1. Follow US 1 north to NC 98 at the town of Wake Forest. Drive about 8 miles to NC 50. Turn right onto NC 50 and travel north 1 mile to the park office/information center, which is on the right just before the bridge. To get to the Woodland Nature Trail, instead of turning into the park, continue north on NC 50, over the bridge, for 2 more miles. Turn left at the Sandling Beach State Recreation Area sign and drive to picnic area 1.

The Sandling Beach State Recreation Area is one of the individual parks that make up the Falls Lake State Recreation Area. The beach sits on Falls Lake in Wake and Durham Counties. The main attraction here is the 12,000-acre lake, which is popular for fishing, swimming, and boating. The 26,000 acres of forested land provide ample opportunity for hiking if you are in the area with your dog.

The Woodland Nature Trail is a little, wooded gem that is located near picnic area 1. It is a nice, shaded leg-stretcher hike that you can take after a swim or a picnic. The area is relatively quiet and peaceful, away from most of the motorboat noise from Falls Lake's other recreation areas. Another plus is the easy access to flush toilets and water fountains. The trail is not heavily traveled and is not open to mountain bikes. Abundant wildflowers in spring and colorful autumn leaves, as well as cooler temperatures and fewer insects, also make it a nice hike in those seasons. However, the Sandling Beach section is closed from November 1 through March 15.

Start the Woodland Nature Trail by crossing the road from the parking area, going away from the lake, and entering the woods at the trailhead sign. Pick up a trail brochure in the box and enter a shady forest of loblolly and Virginia pines. The loop trail has twenty-four numbered posts that point out different natural features, which are described in the booklet. It is not necessary to follow these, but it is an easy natural history lesson that makes the trail more fun. The first post you come to describes the growth of the current woodlands in an area that used to be farmland. At about 400 feet, come to a fork, just after signpost 2, and bear to the right to follow the numbers in sequential order as you walk the loop trail.

At 0.1 mile, arrive at signpost 6, which describes the star-shaped sweet gum tree, one of the hardwood species that start to dominate

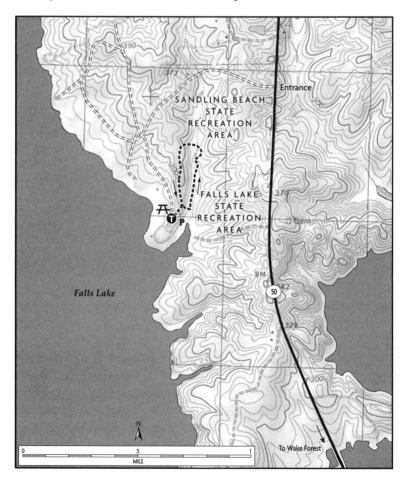

Ellen and Blanca take a rest with Jessie, an Australian yellow heeler, on the Woodland Nature Trail.

a forest as it returns to life (or matures) after farming has ceased. The tree's little, round, red, gumball-shaped fruit can be seen scattered on the ground—just follow your dog's nose to help you spot them. But the tree is actually named not for the fruit but for the sap that used to be chewed as medicine. This is just one of the many natural history tidbits the trail has to offer. If you need a place to contemplate, benches are scattered along the trail.

At 0.3 mile, bear left and ascend steps up a hillside. Wind through the woods on a gently sloping path among the tall pines, southern red oaks, red maples, sourwoods, tulip poplars, beeches, and hickories overhead, as well as a lot for dogs to sniff and explore on the ground, including running cedar, berry bushes, and Christmas ferns.

At 0.7 mile, you are back at the close of the loop. Turn right here and head back to the parking area.

50. Beady Loop Trail—Neuse River Recreation Area, Croatan National Forest

Loop: 1.75 miles
Hiking time: 1 hour
Best time to hike: Fall, winter, and spring
High point: 33 feet
Elevation gain: 30 feet
Difficulty: Easy
Rules and fees: Dogs must be on a leash 6 to 10 feet long
Maps: USGS Havelock; Neuse River Recreation Area
Contact: Croatan National Forest, 252-638-5628; *www.cs.unca.edu/nfsnc*

Getting there: From New Bern, take US 70 east (traveling south) for about 12 miles. Turn left on NC 1107 at the Neuse River Recreation Area sign and drive about 1.5 miles to the parking area.

The Beady Loop Trail is a nice little surprise for dogs and their people who are camping in the Neuse River Recreation Area (known locally as Flanner Beach), which is part of the Croatan National Forest. Hunting and fishing are the primary recreational activities in this small national forest, comprising 160,000 acres between New Bern to the north, Havelock and the Neuse River to the east, the Bogue Sound to the south, and Maysville and the White Oak River to the west. However, hiking trails suitable for dogs here make for especially nice outdoor activity in spring and fall when the weather is cooler and less humid and fewer annoying insects are present. In fact, although this is a great place in summer for people who can camp and swim at the beach, it really is not suitable for dogs then due to high temperatures and the ticks, deerflies, and mosquitoes that proliferate, as well as poisonous snakes.

If you are camping at the 42-site Neuse River Recreation Area, or in the New Bern area in the cooler months, the Beady Loop Trail is a nice woodland stroll for the dogs. Start the trail by entering the woods on a paved path on the right, just before the self-pay station at the campground. (If you are not camping, you do not have to pay to walk the trail). Longleaf

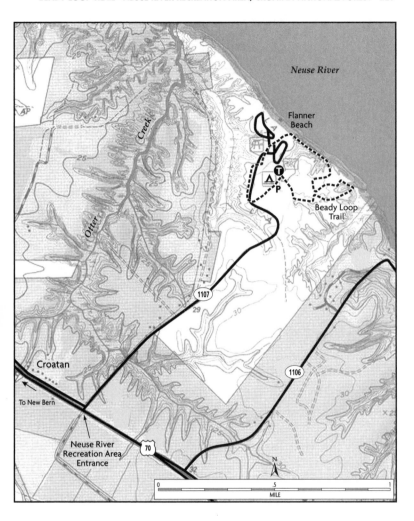

pines, maples, oaks, cedars, and magnolias line the trail. At 0.1 mile, come to a fork and go to the right. Dogs must be on a leash.

At 0.4 mile, arrive at another fork, where you can see some campsites through the trees. Turn right, and then right again, onto a dirt path, and an open area. Soon enter the woods again with many of the same towering trees and an open understory. In spring and fall plenty of wildflowers, ferns, and smells will keep dogs interested as they trot down this peaceful trail.

At about 1.25 miles, you will come to a swampy area on the right with a lot of downed trees. Walk down a little slope into the boggy area and

The Neuse River is visible along sections of the Beady Loop Trail in the Croatan National Forest.

cross over on a boardwalk. You will start to see the river off to the right, through the trees. The trail swings closer to the river, and you can peek out from a couple of places with cuts in the vegetation over the cliffs and down at the river, which is so wide here it looks like the ocean. These are not good places to climb down to the water—the terrain is steep and rocky and not easy for dogs to scramble down, but all the cuts make great perches for checking out the view of the beach, with water lapping like the sea, boats cruising by, and birds swooping.

Continue on the dirt trail, lined in berry bushes and other shrubbery, and wildflowers such as goldenrod in fall. At 1.6 miles, arrive at an intersection with a paved trail and campsites. Turn right here and follow the pavement back to the trailhead and parking area.

51. Island Creek Forest Walk— Croatan National Forest

Loop: 0.5 mile
Hiking time: 30 minutes
Best time to hike: Fall, winter, and spring
High point: 27 feet
Elevation gain: 17 feet
Difficulty: Easy
Rules and fees: Dogs must be on a leash no longer than 6 feet
Maps: USGS Pollocksville; Croatan National Forest
Contact: Croatan National Forest, 252-638-5628; *www.cs.unca .edu/nfsnc*

Getting there: From New Bern, take US 70 east, cross the river, and go to the first intersection with Williams Road. Turn right, cross the railroad tracks and at the T intersection with Madam Moores Lane (NC 1004), turn left. Drive about 7 miles and look for the sign for the Island Creek Forest Walk and a small parking area on the right. (A self-guiding brochure for the walk is available at the Croatan National Forest district office, 10 miles south of New Bern on US 70.)

The Island Creek Forest Walk is probably the smallest hike in the state's second-smallest national forest—the Croatan. North Carolina's eastern-most forest consists of 160,000 acres bordered on three sides by water, including the Neuse, Trent, White Oak, and Newport rivers, and by Bogue Sound, which separates it from the Atlantic Ocean. The forest contains a variety of natural habitats, including freshwater pocosin (meaning "swamp on a hill"), longleaf pine savanna, and saltwater marsh, and is home to a wide range of wildlife, including waterfowl, birds, deer, bears, snakes, and alligators. The area is also known for its population of car-nivorous, or insect-eating, plants, including the pitcher plant and the Venus flytrap. Recreational areas include opportunities for swimming, boating, hunting, fishing, camping, and hiking. Even though this trail is well shaded, it can be a little too warm and mosquito riddled to be fun for dogs in the summer.

The Island Creek Forest Walk, just a few miles outside of downtown New Bern, is a 0.5-mile loop that winds through a forest of pines and

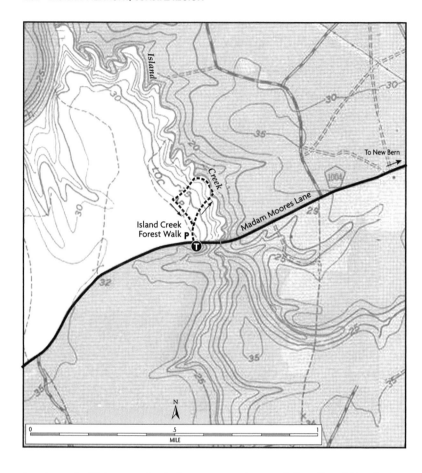

hardwoods. It is a particularly pretty and peaceful trail to hike during spring, with a profusion of wildflowers, and in fall, when the leaf colors are vibrant and the air is on the cooler side.

Enter the forest by the trailhead sign. At 200 feet, where the trail forks, bear to the right to follow the numbered signs in sequence. Following the white rectangular blazes on the trees, you are walking through very lush vegetation, with a softly padded forest floor for the dogs. The dominant trees are the towering loblolly pines, American beeches, yellow poplars, American hollies, dogwoods, sweet gums, and umbrella magnolias, the latter distinctive for their giant-size, fanlike leaves.

At about 0.1 mile, the trail starts to run along Island Creek and follows it for a little while. The water is dark and muddy, and rock ledges overhang the creek in places. These rock outcrops contain fossilized seashells known as marl, deposited millions of years ago when the area was buried beneath the ocean.

While all of that is of interest to people, the dogs will want to splash around in the creek. This water is not suitable for dogs to drink, but there are places for them to get their paws and noses wet. The shady, moist environment is the perfect incubator for a variety of mushrooms, wildflowers, shrubs, and mounds of Christmas ferns. These long evergreen ferns take their name from the shape of their leaflets, which resemble Christmas stockings. Especially in spring when wildflowers are blooming, there is plenty to keep dogs' noses occupied on ground level.

Continue to wind around the loop, looking carefully for the numbered posts. The trail is not hard to follow, but the posts can get lost in the foliage. At 0.5 mile, just after the last post—number 15, describing the red oak tree—you will arrive back at the original intersection. Bear right to finish the loop.

Christmas ferns grow profusely along the Island Creek Forest Walk.

APPENDIX

Hiking/Trail Maintenance Organizations
Following are some trail maintenance groups that work in North Carolina:

Appalachian Trail Conservancy
799 Washington Street
P.O. Box 807
Harpers Ferry, WV 25425-0807
Phone: 304-535-6331
www.appalachiantrail.org

Carolina Mountain Club
P.O. Box 68
Asheville, NC 28802
www.carolinamtnclub.org

**Environmental and
Conservation Organization**
121 Third Avenue West
Suite 4
Hendersonville, NC 28792
Phone: 828-692-0385
www.eco-wnc.org

Friends of DuPont Forest
Brevard, NC Division of
Forest Resources
P.O. Box 300
Cedar Mountain, NC 28718
Phone: 828-877-6527
www.dupontforest.com

**Friends of the
Mountains-to-Sea Trail**
3585 US 401 South
Louisburg, NC 27549
www.ncmst.org

High Country Hikers
P.O. Box 472, Flat Rock, NC 28731
Phone: 828-694-1482
http://main.nc.us/highcountryhikers

Nantahala Hiking Club
173 Carl Slagle Road
Franklin, NC 28734

**National Park Service
Volunteers in Parks**
Blue Ridge Parkway, Asheville, NC
Phone: 828-271-4779
www.nps.gov/blri

**North Carolina Bartram
Trail Society**
P. O. Box 968
Highlands, NC 28741
www.ncbartramtrail.org

The Umstead Coalition
P.O. Box 10654
Raleigh, NC 27605-0654
Phone: 919-852-2268
www.umsteadcoalition.org
info@umsteadcoalition.org

USDA Forest Service
160 Zillicoa Street, Suite A
Asheville, NC 28801
Phone: 828-257-4200
www.cs.unca.edu/nfsnc

INDEX

ABOUT THE AUTHOR

Karen Chávez has lived in the mountains of western North Carolina with her black lab, Shelby, since 2000. She is an editor for the *Asheville Citizen-Times* newspaper, directing coverage of outdoor recreation, environmental, and health and fitness issues. Karen is also editor of *WNC Mountain Travel Guide,* a twice-yearly magazine-style visitor's guide, and has published many articles over the past decade on hiking, hiking with dogs, outdoor recreation, and outdoor sports. Karen has a degree in environmental studies from the State University of New York at Binghamton and a master's degree in journalism from the University of Montana. She is a former ranger with the National Park Service.

Karen and Shelby take a picture break at Price Lake along the Blue Ridge Parkway.

THE MOUNTAINEERS, founded in 1906, is a nonprofit outdoor activity and conservation club, whose mission is "to explore, study, preserve, and enjoy the natural beauty of the outdoors. . . . " Based in Seattle, Washington, the club is now the third-largest such organization in the United States, with seven branches throughout Washington State.

The Mountaineers sponsors both classes and year-round outdoor activities in the Pacific Northwest, which include hiking, mountain climbing, ski-touring, snowshoeing, bicycling, camping, kayaking, nature study, sailing, and adventure travel. The club's conservation division supports environmental causes through educational activities, sponsoring legislation, and presenting informational programs.

All club activities are led by skilled, experienced instructors, who are dedicated to promoting safe and responsible enjoyment and preservation of the outdoors.

If you would like to participate in these organized outdoor activities or the club's programs, consider a membership in The Mountaineers. For information and an application, write or call The Mountaineers, Club Headquarters, 300 Third Avenue West, Seattle, WA 98119; 206-284-6310. You can also visit the club's website at *www.mountaineers.org* or contact The Mountaineers via email at *clubmail@mountaineers.org*.

The Mountaineers Books, an active, nonprofit publishing program of the club, produces guidebooks, instructional texts, historical works, natural history guides, and works on environmental conservation. All books produced by The Mountaineers Books fulfill the club's mission.

Send or call for our catalog of more than 500 outdoor titles:

The Mountaineers Books
1001 SW Klickitat Way, Suite 201
Seattle, WA 98134
800-553-4453
mbooks@mountaineersbooks.org
www.mountaineersbooks.org

The Mountaineers Books is proud to be a corporate sponsor of The Leave No Trace Center for Outdoor Ethics, whose mission is to promote and inspire responsible outdoor recreation through education, research, and partnerships. The Leave No Trace program is focused specifically on human-powered (nonmotorized) recreation.

Leave No Trace strives to educate visitors about the nature of their recreational impacts, as well as offer techniques to prevent and minimize such impacts. Leave No Trace is best understood as an educational and ethical program, not as a set of rules and regulations.

For more information, visit *www.LNT.org*, or call 800-332-4100.

OTHER TITLES YOU MIGHT ENJOY FROM
THE MOUNTAINEERS BOOKS

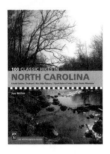
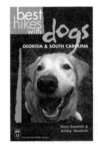

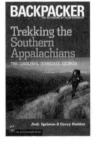